theatre & dramaturgy

Theatre &
Series Editors: Jen Harvie and Dan Rebellato

Published
Natalie Álvarez: *Theatre & War*
Joel Anderson: *Theatre & Photography*
Vicky Angelaki: *Theatre & Environment*
Susan Bennett: *Theatre & Museums*
Bill Blake: *Theatre & the Digital*
Marvin Carlson: *Theatre & Islam*
Colette Conroy: *Theatre & the Body*
Emma Cox: *Theatre & Migration*
Jim Davis: *Theatre & Entertainment*
Jill Dolan: *Theatre & Sexuality*
Kate Elswit: *Theatre & Dance*
Emine Fisek: *Theatre & Community*
Helen Freshwater: *Theatre & Audience*
Jen Harvie: *Theatre & the City*
Nadine Holdsworth: *Theatre & Nation*
Erin Hurley: *Theatre & Feeling*
Dominic Johnson: *Theatre & the Visual*
Joe Kelleher: *Theatre & Politics*
Ric Knowles: *Theatre & Interculturalism*
David Kornhaber: *Theatre & Knowledge*
Petra Kuppers: *Theatre & Disability*
Margherita Laera: *Theatre & Translation*
Yair Lipshitz: *Theatre & Judaism*
Brian Lobel: *Theatre & Cancer*
Patrick Lonergan: *Theatre & Social Media*
Caoimhe McAvinchey: *Theatre & Prison*
Bruce McConachie: *Theatre & Mind*
Lucy Nevitt: *Theatre & Violence*
Helen Nicholson: *Theatre & Education*
Lourdes Orozco: *Theatre & Animals*
Lionel Pilkington: *Theatre & Ireland*
Benjamin Poore: *Theatre & Empire*
Paul Rae: *Theatre & Human Rights*
Alan Read: *Theatre & Law*
Dan Rebellato: *Theatre & Globalization*
Trish Reid: *Theatre & Scotland*
Nicholas Ridout: *Theatre & Ethics*
Jo Robinson: *Theatre & The Rural*
Mark Robson: *Theatre & Death*
Juliet Rufford: *Theatre & Architecture*
Elizabeth Schafer: *Theatre & Christianity*
Rebecca Schneider: *Theatre & History*
Lara Shalson: *Theatre & Protest*
Kim Solga: *Theatre & Feminism*
Konstantinos Thomaidis: *Theatre & Voice*
Fintan Walsh: *Theatre & Therapy*
Eric Weitz: *Theatre & Laughter*
David Wiles: *Theatre & Time*
Harvey Young: *Theatre & Race*
Keren Zaiontz: *Theatre & Festivals*

theatre & dramaturgy

Zoë Svendsen

methuen | drama

LONDON • NEW YORK • OXFORD • NEW DELHI • SYDNEY

METHUEN DRAMA
Bloomsbury Publishing Plc
50 Bedford Square, London, WC1B 3DP, UK
1385 Broadway, New York, NY 10018, USA
29 Earlsfort Terrace, Dublin 2, Ireland

BLOOMSBURY, METHUEN DRAMA and the Methuen Drama logo are trademarks of
Bloomsbury Publishing Plc

First published in Great Britain 2023
Copyright © Zoë Svendsen, 2023
Series Editors' Preface © Jen Harvie and Dan Rebellato, 2023

For legal purposes the Acknowledgements on p. xiii constitute an extension
of this copyright page.

Series design by Liron Gilenberg | www.ironicitalics.com
Cover design by Gita Govinda Kowlessur
Cover image © yodiyim/ iStock

A catalogue record for this book is available from the British Library.

A catalog record for this book is available from the Library of Congress.

ISBN: PB: 978-1-3503-3246-1
    ePDF: 978-1-3503-3247-8
    eBook: 978-1-3503-3248-5

Series: Theatre &

Typeset by Deanta Global Publishing Services, Chennai, India
Printed and bound in Great Britain

To find out more about our authors and books visit www.bloomsbury.com and
sign up for our newsletters.

contents

Series editors' preface		vii
Foreword		ix
Theatre & thanks		xiii
Introduction		1
	What is dramaturgy?	1
	Dramaturgy and drama	3
	Dramaturgical approaches	8
	Dramaturgy and plays	10
	Dramaturgy and production	12
1	Dramaturgy and the audience	15
	Dramaturgies of entertainment	16
	Acting 'for' the audience	18
	Theatricality	20
	Dramaturgies of autonomy	23
	Modernism	23
	Ignoring the audience	25

	Autonomy and absorption	26
	Legacies of Modernism	29
	A comforting convention?	32
	Dramaturgies of the political	35
	Naturalism	36
	The epic theatre	39
	Brecht's legacy	41
	Get out of the theatre (and into performance)	42
	Dramaturgies of participation	48
	A plethora of forms	49
	Participation and politics	51
2	Dramaturgy and power	54
	Dramaturgy and economy	54
	Dramaturgies of winners and losers	57
	Critiquing racial capitalism	61
	Dramaturgy and marginalization	62
	Dramaturgy and representation	66
	Dramaturgies of imagining otherwise	72
	Theatre and climate crisis	77
	Coda	86
	Further reading	89
	Index	99

series editors' preface

The theatre is everywhere, from entertainment districts to the fringes, from the rituals of government to the ceremony of the courtroom, from the spectacle of the sporting arena to the theatres of war. Across these many forms stretches a theatrical continuum through which cultures both assert and question themselves.

Theatre has been around for thousands of years, and the ways we study it have changed decisively. It's no longer enough to limit our attention to the canon of Western dramatic literature. Theatre has taken its place within a broad spectrum of performance, connecting it with the wider forces of ritual and revolt that thread through so many spheres of human culture. In turn, this has helped make connections across disciplines; over the past fifty years, theatre and performance have been deployed as key metaphors and practices with which to rethink gender, economics, war, language, the fine arts, culture and one's sense of self.

Theatre & is a long series of short books which hopes to capture the restless interdisciplinary energy of theatre and performance. Each book explores connections between theatre and some aspect of the wider world, asking how the theatre might illuminate the world and how the world might illuminate the theatre. Each book is written by a leading theatre scholar and represents the cutting edge of critical thinking in the discipline.

We have been mindful, however, that the philosophical and theoretical complexity of much contemporary academic writing can act as a barrier to a wider readership. A key aim for these books is that they should all be readable in one sitting by anyone with a curiosity about the subject. The books are challenging, pugnacious, visionary sometimes and, above all, clear. We hope you enjoy them.

Jen Harvie and Dan Rebellato

foreword

Does it work? This question resounds around every rehearsal room and can refer to any aspect of the text or performance and, indeed, the whole play. The real test, we say, is in front of an audience, then we will find out if what we intended is working as we intended it. *Theatre & Dramaturgy* makes the point that practitioners rarely name this as 'dramaturgy' but that is exactly what it is. So we're all doing it. In Shakespeare's *Midsummer Night's Dream* the Mechanicals show us dramaturgy in action. Bottom the weaver is warned that roaring too loudly as the lion will cause them all to be hanged, so he declares, 'I will roar you as/ gently as any sucking dove, I will roar you/ an t'were any nightingale' (Act I, sc. 2). Of course, as they perform the play, their metatheatrical audience sniggers while we, the real audience, roar. Their failure is Shakespeare's triumph because he knew what he was doing, but for me, an audience laughing at a play instead of with it can feel very bad indeed and would be a clear example of the failure of the dramaturgical process. But dramaturgy is more than getting it right. It is the very strategy that is used to structure the audience's relation to the work they are encountering.

I began as a practitioner in the 1980s with a women's theatre collective called Resisters: we insisted on gender, race, sexuality and class inclusivity and just representation. We resisted the well-made play that had put the white, middle class, heteronormative male centre stage. We wanted to reach audiences that may have been excluded from traditional bourgeois theatre and so we performed in community spaces. As a result we required a new dramaturgy, which allowed us to address our new audience directly, using diverse elements, cabaret, song, political sketches, poetry and putting women centre stage, to put our revolutionary points across.

I wrote *Playhouse Creatures* in 1993, based on the history of the first English actresses.

I had been an actress myself but it had previously never crossed my mind to ask questions about when women had first been allowed to act. I decided to frame the play in a ghostly world of an abandoned theatre so as to emphasize that this ignored, lost story was still marginalized by our culture. Sphinx Theatre company debated the meaning of this framing. Was it necessary to the story? Would an audience 'get it'? It became clear through the early performances that what had seemed problematic was readily accepted by the audience and did indeed highlight the fragility of this rediscovered history. Then we couldn't imagine the play without it.

Every time a playwright sits down to write a play they are faced with the what (content) and the how (form). *Theatre & Dramaturgy* does the brilliant job of illuminating and clarifying the process of making work by throwing its emphasis on what is being asked of the *audience*.

How are *they* positioned in relation to the work? How is *their* attention structured? It examines what political choices we make, both intentional and unintentional, when we choose our forms and methods of engagement with audiences. It does this by unfolding the history of our culture's dramaturgical choices with great examples and persuasive clarity. It's an invigorating journey looking at different forms and their varying relationships to the audience, analyzing dramaturgy as relations of power from the perspective of the global majority, feminism, class perspectives and LBGTQ communities.

Placing plays in the context of their dramaturgy allows for very productive readings of plays and theatre. The Restoration theatre was a social place and the dramaturgy depended on charismatic performances, with actors connecting to the audience (Dramaturgy of Entertainment). Plays in the modernist tradition can be seen as a rebellion against capitalism, sealing themselves off from the audience in order to resist the notion of selling themselves. Brecht resisted this immersion in the individual (Dramaturgy of Autonomy) and called for a dramaturgy that highlighted social being as determining thought (Political Dramaturgy).

Theatre & Dramaturgy deconstructs the choices playwrights and theatre practitioners have made, putting them in their cultural and social context with an emphasis on power relations; this makes for a fresh and insightful analysis and is fundamentally empowering, both as an audience member and for any playwright or theatre practitioner making work, because it makes clear the political nature of the dramaturgical decisions we make and offers us a perspective from which to make more radical decisions.

As a playwright *Theatre & Dramaturgy* is a totally essential must-read.

April De Angelis
December, 2022

theatre & thanks

My heartfelt thanks to Jen Harvie, whose guidance, wisdom and detailed feedback were invaluable; and also to Dom O'Hanlon and Dan Rebellato for the commission and care; to all the writers and directors at the Royal Court and Young Vic respectively who took part in workshops discussing early drafts and to Jane Fallowfield and Sue Emmas for organizing this; to my current and former students, undergraduate and graduate, at the University of Cambridge, who have engaged in multiple classes and conversations on these questions; to April de Angelis, Rachel Taylor and Charlie Josephine for their dramaturgical insights and encouragement; to Hélène Brunerie and Naz Simsek for their meticulous attention to detail when acting as my computer eyes at various stages; to Kate Raworth, Ha-Joon Chang and Paul Mason for my economics education; to the directors with whom I've collaborated over the past decade as dramaturg: Joe Hill-Gibbins, Polly Findlay, Sean Holmes,

Abigail Graham and Clint Dyer; to Clare Slater and resident assistant directors Josh Parr and Dadiow Lin at the Donmar Warehouse for their support and engagement with climate dramaturgy; to the New Wolsey's Sarah Holmes and Pete Rowe for their mentorship; to Emily Mclaughlin, and to Lucy Kerbel of Tonic Theatre and the Advance programme, for the conversations around gender and representation; to David Lan for enabling my work as dramaturg and director; to international collaborators Uta Lindner, Luk Perceval, Christian Tschirner, Imanuel Schipper, Cecilie Sachs Olsen and many others; to Hilary Seaward for making METIS possible; to my many creative collaborators of the last decade, especially Simon Daw, and including Rob Awosusi, Nicky Childs, Naomi Christie, Carolyn Downing, Shôn Dale-Jones, Lucy Ellinson, Charlie Folorunsho, Guy Hoare, Jess Mabel Jones, Heather Lai, Andrea Ling, Jamie Martin, Stefanie Mueller, Anna-Maria Nabirye, Nao Nagai, Kate O'Connor, Tom Ross-Williams, Steve Wald and Lucy Wray. And personally, to Leo Mellor for all your encouragement and reading of drafts, to my children Max and Tom, and to my parents, Penny and David Svendsen.

introduction

> *It matters what thoughts think thoughts. It matters what*
> *knowledges know knowledges. It matters what relations relate*
> *relations. It matters what worlds world worlds. It matters what*
> *stories tell stories.*
>
> (Donna J. Haraway, *Staying with the Trouble*, 2016, p. 35)

What is dramaturgy?

In the preface to *Theatre & Feeling*, director Anne Bogart describes the way that emotion is not inherent *in* a work of theatre but is produced *by* it: 'feeling is a by-product of a precise arrangement of circumstances' (2010, p. x). Dramaturgy is that 'arrangement'. And in being about how all the elements of theatre are held in relation to one another, it is both everything in theatre and nothing in particular – this book could almost be called *Theatre & Theatre*. And yet: dramaturgy perhaps needs its own address most of all precisely because it is the formal dimension of theatre with which theatre people work all the time, but is rarely named, subsumed in pragmatic discussions of 'what works'. Many of the elements that constitute dramaturgy appear so self-evident that they barely merit scrutiny, because they are familiar – yet it is the specific relationships *between* these elements in any given performance that create its dramaturgy and thereby both produce its emotional effect and express the work's politics.

Dramaturgy is specific to theatre, because dramaturgy involves a basic theatrical condition – the relation between the watched and the watcher. It is one of the few essential elements of theatre, as director Peter Brook indicates in his famous opening to *The Empty Space* (1968):

> I can take any empty space and call it a bare stage. A man [*sic*] walks across this empty space whilst someone else is watching him, and this is all that is needed for an act of theatre to be engaged. (p. 11)

What I would add is that the action is presumed by the spectator to be an act of representation (even if that representation is indistinguishable from what it 'is' – the simple act of a man walking). Dramaturgy, then, forms what I call a 'structure of attention', holding and directing the attention of the audience. I therefore define dramaturgy as follows:

> Dramaturgy is the arranging of representational actions in relation to space and time, orientated towards establishing a relationship with an audience.

After giving an overview of dramaturgy's history in this introduction, the book is split into two parts. Part 1, 'Dramaturgy and the Audience', uses a historical lens to explore how plays and productions position their audiences in relation to the work and how that affects their meaning. Part 2, 'Dramaturgy and Power', takes a different approach, examining dramaturgy through thinking about forms of social, political and economic power. This part explores how dramaturgies construct meaning, suggesting that relations of power are embedded in the dramaturgical form of the work – even when not explicitly recognized by audiences. The second part concludes by asking what role dramaturgy might have to play in the coming times. Throughout, I offer examples of specific plays or performances – and increasingly turn to questions of politics.

Dramaturgy and drama

Dramaturgy is a European concept that was invented in Germany in the late 1700s. The eighteenth-century Enlightenment dramatist, philosopher and art critic Gottfried Abraham Lessing drew on the ancient Greek words for 'action' and 'working together' to produce the word 'dramaturgy'. This described an artistic and social practice that would create, in the words of Bernd Stegemann, the former head dramaturg of Berlin's Schaubühne: 'A different and new relationship between the audience and the theatre' ('On German Dramaturgy', 2014, p. 45).

From the start, exploring dramaturgy was a practical endeavour, an activity of making and modelling ways of doing theatre. Lessing set up the Hamburg National Theatre in 1767, becoming the first 'dramaturg'. Although the theatre struggled financially and had to close after three years, the idea of dramaturgy persisted; today, every civic theatre in Germany has a 'dramaturgy' department, responsible for the theatre's programme of performances, casting and shaping texts for performance as well as collaborating with directors and creative teams to stage productions. This is the case across most of continental Europe, whereas in the United Kingdom and the United States, the history of the theatre industry has been more commercial than civic, affecting how theatre defines itself. Broadly speaking, the consideration of dramaturgy goes hand in hand with a European approach to theatre that is analytical and critical, centring on artistic expression and social commentary.

Dramaturgy implies, in the very word, a relationship to drama. Before I start to tease out the relationships between text, action, performance, space, time and meaning that produce a theatre work's dramaturgy, it feels important to articulate what I understand by the term 'drama'. This is a culturally specific understanding of the term – related to the history of theatre in Europe, where I am situated. In this, I draw on the German tradition, which in turn draws on the ancient Greek understanding of dramatic representation as the 'imitation of a complete, i.e. whole, action', as described by the ancient Greek philosopher Aristotle (*Poetics*, 1996, p. 13). 'Drama' was first used as a term in English in the early sixteenth century, derived from Greek (via Latin). The first dramas, performed in cycles as part of ancient Greek religious rituals and involving the (male) civic community, are often discussed by historians in dramaturgical terms, identifying the distinction of an individual actor from the group of the chorus, enabling representation of a character, separate from the chorus' narrative description. Aristotle describes how the dramatist Aeschylus introduced a second actor, in addition to the chorus, allowing for the possibility of dialogue, and later the dramatist Sophocles introduced a third actor (p. 8). There were never more than three characters on stage at any one time, although the three actors, wearing masks, would usually play more than one character in different scenes (P. E. Easterling, *The Cambridge Companion to Greek Tragedy*, 1997, pp. 151–3). In addition, there were around fifteen members of a chorus who commented on the action – and set it in a wider mythological context.

In Renaissance Italy, and later in France, translations of Aristotle's works resulted in playwrights following specific dramaturgical rules, described as the three classical unities of drama. These were: unity of action – that is, a single plot; unity of place – the story takes place in one location; and unity of time – the story unfolds over a timescale equivalent to real time. In the eighteenth century, European Enlightenment playwrights and philosophers further emphasized individual agency. For example, the German philosopher Friedrich Hegel described dramatic action as 'emanating from the inner life of a self-directed character and as determined in its outcome by the substantial nature of purposes, individuals and collisions' ('Tragedy as a Dramatic Art', p. 1).

Drama tells a story by representing interpersonal relationships through the medium of dialogue – that is, by means of representing people talking to one another. In this context, what tends to sustain audiences' attention over time is the question of why the character acts thus (the cause) and *how that action might affect others*. Most importantly, action's place at the heart of drama implies a fundamental belief in humans as *agents*, as capable of altering each other and the world around them. In the late nineteenth century, the Russian theatre director Konstantin Stanislavski developed a rehearsal system centred on characters acting in a future-orientated, intentional manner to bring about change in themselves or others' situations. This system had an enormous impact across Europe and the United States, spawning a wide variety of theories and practices, which remain highly influential today.

Drama is not, then, completely synonymous with the idea of a play: plays have many extra-dramatic elements, features that involve forms of representation other than dialogue between characters. For example, there are many examples of narrators in plays, from Shakespeare's *The Winter's Tale* (1611) to Tennessee Williams' *Glass Menagerie* (1944). Narrators in plays might disrupt the action, offer information that troubles the apparent meaning of a scene, or bridge a temporal or geographic gap between one part of the action and another. Their function is, importantly, separate from the drama itself. For the same reason, the soliloquy, chorus, aside, prologue and epilogue are not essential to drama but may be an element in a play's dramaturgy.

Understanding dramaturgy as naming how all elements that make up a performance are held in relation to one another, regardless of their relationship to drama, is crucial. It allows what began as a European concept to be rethought in different cultural contexts while inviting those embedded in European cultures to recognize the cultural specificity of how dramaturgy is presumed to relate to drama. As long as there is an imagined or actual spectator, a performer and a prearranged set of representational actions (whether produced through rehearsal or by agreeing a set of rules), which are then performed in front of spectator(s), then the work can be said to have a dramaturgy. This definition also moves beyond the kinds of distinction between types of theatre produced in arguments around supposed 'active' or 'passive' spectatorship, or arguments around the politics of 'participation', which I will turn to at the end of Part 1.

Although the dramaturgy of every work of theatre is different, there are some tacitly assumed 'norms' that govern how audiences expect their attention to be held in the theatres of industrial modernity. This is theatre that emerged in the European and North American cultures of industrial and colonial supremacy, from the late nineteenth century to the present. In the contemporary theatre, a plethora of other kinds of dramaturgy are tacitly defined against these 'norms' – implicit in descriptions like 'avant-garde', 'experimental', 'alternative', 'political' or 'physical', or sometimes in the comment that a performance work is 'not really a play/drama/theatre'. More than a century has seen wave after wave of 'avant-garde' practices influence theatre without displacing the dominant mode of defining these practices as 'other'. However, defining a range of dramaturgies as 'other' to a 'norm' can reinforce the marginalization of those dramaturgies, particularly if that 'norm' – the conventions and assumptions underlying the distinction – are not discussed. This book therefore aims to reveal the workings of the kinds of dramaturgy that audiences in Western industrial countries take for granted, in order to unpick those assumptions and reveal the powerful social constructs behind them.

Dramaturgical approaches

These are some questions that thinking dramaturgically might lead you to ask of a performance work:

- How are the audience positioned (politically, socially, architecturally) in relation to the structure of the work?
- What rules are conventional, and what are established by the work/specific environment the performance takes place in?
- How much of the work's internal structure is left to be determined through decisions/input from the audience?
- How far does the dramaturgy involve fictional or other kinds of representation?

In the introduction to their excellent *New Dramaturgy: International Perspectives on Theory and Practice* (2014), Katalin Trencsényi and Bernadette Cochrane discuss the wide variety of terms used for different kinds of dramaturgy in scholarship and performance practice. This book, alongside Magda Romanska's comprehensive *The Routledge Companion to Dramaturgy* (2014), brings together the leading thinkers in the field, reflecting on an area of scholarship and practice that has blossomed in the English-speaking world over the past decade, often fostered by scholars and dramaturgs of European origin. In the rest of Europe, indeed, dramaturgy is a long-established field of practice and research, while it is only since the millennium that the role of dramaturg has become more common in the UK. Dramaturgy as an idea and practice remains, however, obscure to most theatregoers.

This is partly because the role of dramaturg is highly varied, dependent on the context of production and shaped by specific relationships with directors and other members of the creative team (Anne Cattaneo, *The Art of Dramaturgy*, 2021). This book focuses instead on what dramaturgy *is* and what it *does* in terms of how it structures audiences' attention, drawing on my practical experience as dramaturg and director, in a range of British and European contexts. Therefore, most of the examples in this book are from the British theatre, alongside European and American theatre where it has had international impact. It offers an array of examples that illuminate elements of dramaturgy that I hope you will be able to see echoed or reframed in your own context. On the one hand, I've worked as writer/ director/maker with a wide variety of collaborators to create mid- to large-scale participatory works that confront contemporary political subjects from consumer capitalism to climate change. On the other, I have worked as dramaturg with a variety of directors in the British subsidized theatre, at institutions such as the Royal Shakespeare Company and, in London, the Young Vic, the National Theatre, the outdoor Globe and indoor Sam Wanamaker Playhouse (which recreates the architecture of the playhouses of Shakespeare's era). I draw on those experiences to explore the way that dramaturgy not only determines the aesthetic of any given theatre work but also encodes a politics, whether declared or not; as the scholar Donna J. Haraway points out (as quoted at the start of this book), 'it matters what relations relate relations' (*Staying with the Trouble*, 2016, p. 35). In other words, the arrangement of elements in time, space and the relation to the audience (included, excluded, immersed, dispersed) that composes a work's dramaturgy are relations of power.

Dramaturgy and plays

To give some ideas of the specific aspects you might explore when reading a play and trying to understand how it works dramaturgically, here are a few of the structural elements you might look at.

- Number and length of scenes and how much they vary – this will give you a sense of the rhythm of the play.
- How many characters – and how many characters in each scene – and how this varies. This will give you a sense of what kind of world is being represented (a play

with fewer characters tends to focus more on individual psychology).

- The implied nature of the stage space – is it a precise location? Are there many locations? This will give you a sense of how the play is attempting to represent the world – e.g. metaphorically or realistically, as a social space or a psychological space, or a combination.
- The extent and type of stage directions (i.e. how precise or provocative the writer is with regard to the spatiality, visual and gestural dimensions of the play as it is imagined for performance).
- Whether the play has a linear time frame or switches between different time frames.
- How it handles its narrative or narratives (whether there is one central narrative or several subplots and how they relate to one another) or whether it resists narrative.
- The relationship between plot and story (plot being the sequence of what happens on stage, story being the sequence of events that take place in the world of the play, which may or may not be shown on stage).
- Whether the dialogue is composed of short or long sentences or speeches – or whether this varies between characters or between/within scenes, and how it sounds, rhythmically, as a result.
- At what point in the play the main events (actions or revelations) take place – for example, does it build towards a revelation, or does the play explore what happens in the wake of an event affecting the figures represented.

- Numbers of exits and entrances – how 'busy' is the stage action?

Consideration of these questions will determine the genre of the play; for example, a farce characteristically has a mid-sized cast and many entrances and exits. Dramaturgical elements are often embedded in the very text of the play; some will be gestured to in stage directions, and many can be – and often are – adapted or altered in the process of staging a production of the play.

Dramaturgy and production

The dramaturgy of a play is the compositional arrangement of the writing in its orientation towards performance. However, dramaturgy need not, of course, start with (or result in) a play-text; in fact one of the most energized developments in dramaturgy from the 1990s onwards has been in dance dramaturgy. The dramaturgy of a play-text and the dramaturgy of that play's production are not identical: production dramaturgy must take into account lighting, sound, silence, bodily presence (or absence) and scenic design – that is, how all the elements of theatre come together to create a performance. Many productions of plays seek to use these features of theatre to express the dramaturgy of the play as they interpret it to have been intended by the writer. However, across the later twentieth century and into the twenty-first century, many practitioners became disillusioned with the idea of drama as an adequate means to express contemporary experience. With the postmodern collapse of the idea of 'grand narrative' – a term used to describe the sense that there is an overarching purpose to life – in response to an increasingly mediatized, globalized world, many theatre makers have felt that the central premise of drama, that of an individual agent able to bring about change, no longer applies.

This has given rise to an important strand of late-twentieth-century theatre, termed 'post-dramatic theatre' by German scholar Hans-Thies Lehmann, which describes features of production dramaturgies that actively break with drama and mimetic representation. Lehmann's seminal book, *Postdramatic Theatre* (2006; first published in German in 1999), anatomizes the many and varied dramaturgical features of post-dramatic theatre, so I won't go into detail here. However, one way of recognizing post-dramatic theatre is to explore how far a production works against the dramaturgical suppositions of classical drama – either by remodelling a classical text or by eschewing conventional modes of narrative and representation. Although Lehmann characterizes post-dramatic theatre as a distinctly *theatrical* phenomenon, displacing the primacy of the written word, there is a wide range of playwrights who create dramaturgies that question the central tenets of drama. Such plays often actively demand dramaturgical intervention on the part of the director and actors when staging their work in the theatre, disrupting the idea that the creators of the production are merely presenting the written play in performance. The absence of character designations in, say, Caryl Churchill's *Love and Information* (2012), or Martin

Crimp's *Attempts on Her Life* (1997), or Sarah Kane's *Crave* (1998) or *4:48 Psychosis* (2000), invites – indeed forces – creative teams to create a production dramaturgy that is not 'given' by the play.

However, whether the structural relationship between text, drama, and performance is complementary or provocatively antagonistic, what all dramaturgies have in common is that the theatre work's structure encodes how that work relates to a (potential or actual) audience. This is what makes dramaturgy a specifically *theatrical* phenomenon, and it is what part 1 will explore through a historical lens, focussing on theatre from the late nineteenth century to the present.

1 dramaturgy and the audience

In what follows, I explore three different dramaturgical structures that shape the relationship between art, performance, drama and the audience. First, I explore 'dramaturgies of entertainment', exploring theatricality and the virtuosity of the actor. In the following section, 'dramaturgies of autonomy', I consider 'modern' drama, in which the presence of the audience is denied or excluded in opposition to dramaturgies of entertainment. By 'autonomy', I mean the idea that art is timeless, independent of its creators, as though it were without social context. In 'political dramaturgies', I discuss how political theatre establishes a different relationship with an audience, seeking to change or alter its beliefs and behaviour. What I hope to demonstrate is how plays and performances define their intended relationship with audiences not just through their content but especially through their dramaturgy, with particular reference to styles of acting. In the last section of this part, I turn to what are often called 'open' or 'play' dramaturgies, to explore how interactive and immersive theatre works can also be defined through these three categories of dramaturgical relation with the audience, that is 'entertainment', 'autonomy' or the 'political'. This leads on to a discussion in the second part of the book about the way in which dramaturgies encode relations of power, including in the spaces of theatre making, but also, importantly, beyond them.

Dramaturgies of entertainment

This section identifies a variety of dramaturgical structures that are designed to entertain. Across different kinds of theatre in different eras, they share a common aim in being primarily orientated towards the pleasure of their audiences, often utilizing the theatricality of theatre – its artificiality and glamour – to impress, tease and invite vocal responses. In the eighteenth and nineteenth century, the European theatre was a highly sociable place, with audiences often as interested in one another as what was happening on stage. Huge, grandiose set designs were particularly popular, impressing audiences through visual spectacle rather than drama (Jacky Bratton, 'What Is a Play', 2007, p. 253). In a reaction to this trend, in the late nineteenth century, the French playwright Eugène Scribe coined the term 'la pièce bien faite' or 'well-made play'. The purpose of this dramaturgy, according to mid-twentieth-century critic John Russell Taylor, was to ensure commercial success for the playwright, through creating a dramaturgical structure that would hold the audiences' attention for the duration of the performance:

> [Scribe] saw that all drama, in performance, is an experience in time, and that therefore the first essential is to keep one's audience attentive from one minute to the next. Romantic drama [i.e. of the Victorian era] tended to neglect this requirement, or at least do little to satisfy it. [. . .] His plays inculcated [. . .] the spacing and preparation of effects so that an audience should be kept expectant from beginning to end. (*The Rise and Fall of The Well-Made Play,* 1967, p. 12)

Unlike spectacle, which only impresses in the moment of its revelation, the well-made play used drama, which engages audiences' attention over time. Early-twentieth-century British playwright George Bernard Shaw's definition of the dramaturgy of the well-made play is useful: 'you had in what was called a well-made play an exposition in the first act, a situation in the second, an unravelling in the third' (*The Quintessence of Ibsenism,* 1928, p. 213). The situational conflict is developed through tropes such as accidental or deliberate substitutions, mistaken identities or revelations of secrets (often of a sexual nature). Finally, equilibrium is re-established, restoring order to the situation. The dramatic movement towards resolution in well-made plays at once implies human agency *and* reinforces the status quo. What wasn't known at the start of the play and provides impetus is fully revealed and solved by the end. Such well-made plays populated the European theatres of the nineteenth century: relying on a presumed consensus regarding highly conservative social values for the recognition of heroes, villains, sexual escapades and redemptive acts. Hardly any of the early well-made plays are read or performed today, but it is a form that allies drama and theatricality in ways that have had an all-pervasive influence.

Acting 'for' the audience

Many of the well-made plays that are most frequently revived – or which are based on this form – thematize the theatricality of the actor, pursuing a dramaturgy that requires the actor to demonstrate their prowess and overtly orientate their performance towards the audience. In the twentieth century, playwrights such as Oscar Wilde, Noël Coward, Terence Rattigan and later Alan Ayckbourn, Yasmina Reza and Michael Frayn mastered this form (the comparative lack of female names in this list is perhaps instructive). Oscar Wilde set the tone in the late nineteenth century for marrying effective plots with a subversively self-conscious pleasure in overt theatricality. As a middle-class Irishman writing for the English upper classes, and a gay man writing for a strictly heteronormative, homophobic and generally sexually conservative society, he wrote plays that are brightly artificial in construction, providing actors with plenty of opportunity to play the theatre crowd.

Wilde does not seek to conceal the dramaturgy of the play and in this lies the politics of his writing. The overtly artificial patterning of the plot implicitly satirizes the audience for taking the work more seriously than it takes itself. We are hardly expected to 'believe' in the characters – and indeed, this disregard for plausibility is played up in the way the characters themselves satirize one another's emotional lives.

Take, for example, this exchange in *Lady Windermere's Fan* (1892). Lady Windermere has noticed that her husband is acting in a suspicious way with regard to another woman:

Lord Windermere   Ah, Margaret! Only trust
me! A wife should trust her husband!
Lady Windermere   London is full of women
who trust their husbands. One can always
recognise them. They look so thoroughly unhappy.
(Oscar Wilde, *Plays*, 1978, p. 33)

The events of the plot more or less exist to enable the actors to deliver one-liners such as these, lines which could easily – and frequently – detach from their context in the drama. However, the drama brings depth of feeling to the wit, just as the wit, which offers a different kind of relation between actor and the audience, draws attention to the constructed nature of the situation. The more the actor enjoys playing the lines, the more fully the dramaturgy of the play is realized: the success of the play depends not on the plausibility of the world depicted but on the ability of the actors to share the joke with the audience.

'Well-made' plays thus place the actor's relationship with the act of performing centre stage, explicitly in service to their audiences. The fact that an actor will be acting *for* an audience is embedded as a condition of the craft of writing, and these plays lend themselves to being played in ways that encourage the audience to perceive and enjoy the skill of the actor. The spectators are regarded as the arbiters of taste and acknowledged as the judges of the value of the work, as mid-twentieth-century playwright Terence Rattigan suggests: 'A play can neither be great, nor a masterpiece, nor a work of genius, nor talented, nor untalented, nor indeed anything at all unless it has an audience to see it' (quoted by Noël Coward, *Encore*, 1962, p. 176). This might seem self-evident, but Rattigan made this comment in a post-war context in which, as a master of well-made plays, his work and this attitude to the audience fell out of fashion. The reasons for this will be explored in 'Dramaturgies of autonomy'.

Theatricality

Dramaturgies of entertainment often revel in theatricality: in the overt expression of performance *as* performance. The word 'theatrical' is often used colloquially to describe the fake, deceitful and artificial (in life as well as art), and the long history of anti-theatrical bile testifies to a range of fears – not least regarding the stability of the relationship between representation and what is being represented (see Jonas Barish's history of the hate heaped on theatre, *The Antitheatrical Prejudice*, 1981). What is never far away in anti-theatrical discourse is a latent homophobia, rooted in an anxiety about the stability of sexual and gender categories in theatrical representation.

In Coward's *Design for Living* (1932), he satirizes a theatre culture that disapproves of writing that depends not on immersion in the world of the play but rather on the ability of the actor to sustain an audience's attention. In Act II, scene 1, Leo, a successful playwright, and Gilda, his lover, are reading the newspaper reviews of his new play:

Leo [. . .] the dialogue is polished and sustains a high level from first to last and is frequently witty, nay, even brilliant – '[. . .]' 'But' – here we go, dear! – 'But the play, on the whole, is decidedly thin.' [. . .] *(jumping up)* Thin–thin! What do they mean, 'thin'?

Gilda Just thin, darling. Thin's thin the world over and you can't get away from it.

Leo Would you call it thin?

Gilda Emaciated.

(Act II, scene 1, p. 34)

What *does* 'thin' mean, when applied to a play? An answer of sorts comes in Coward's own description of the response to another of his plays, *Private Lives* (1930), which was

> described in the papers as being 'tenuous', 'thin', 'brittle', 'gossamer', 'iridescent', and 'delightfully daring'. All of which connoted, to the public mind, 'cocktails', 'evening dress', 'repartee', and irreverent allusions to copulation, thereby causing a gratifying number of respectable people to queue up at the box office. ('Introduction', *Plays Two*, 1979, p. xiv)

'Thin', Coward implies, is a result of a dramaturgy focused on the relationship with an audience in performance, rather than on the internal workings of drama. So what holds the play together? According to Coward, it is 'expert technique'; the actors' virtuosity in building rapport with an audience completes the dramaturgy.

When the musical *Tina* (2018), a biopic of singer-songwriter Tina Turner's life, directed by Phyllida Lloyd, transferred from London's West End to Broadway in New York, it was met with a similar response by *The New York Times*, contrasting the quality of the acting with the supposed 'thinness' of the drama (Jesse Green, 'The "Tina" Musical Is One Inch Deep, Mountain High', *The New York Times*, 7 November 2019). In form – a biopic encompassing many of the most famous songs in Turner's back catalogue – it sometimes came close to a concert. Nevertheless, the virtuosity of acting that the production displayed, particularly on the part of Adrienne Warren and Kobna Holdbrook-Smith, was rooted in the text's commitment to telling the story. The pleasure in watching the dexterity of the actors (as praised by the review) move between performance forms was deepened by our investment in character – while allowing the songs to speak for themselves. In this sense, the dramaturgy was precisely designed to enable this virtuosic theatricality and succeeded in doing so, rather than being in some way lacking (as was implied by Green's use of the word 'thinness').

In the early modern period, no such distinction was made: Shakespeare and his contemporaries wrote for a commercial theatre that was entirely dependent on pleasing its audience while also producing what has since been heralded as the greatest poetry in the English language. The next section focuses on dramaturgies that hold a very different relationship with the audience to explore how and why in the modern era, popular entertainment has come to be separated from 'art'.

Dramaturgies of autonomy

In dramaturgies of entertainment, the performer actively attracts attention to themself as an actor, as well as mediating attention towards a fiction: attention is split between the sign (the actor) and what it signifies (the character). Yet 'truth' in acting has come to be allied with the idea of serving the play or production, rather than drawing attention to the actor themselves. Why is the acknowledgement of the presence of the actor in the theatre so enjoyed by some and so troubling to others? An answer, I believe, comes through exploring the influence of the twentieth-century cultural movement of Modernism on attitudes to artistic practice and how this has in turn influenced theatre practice. The next section will explore how – and why – dramaturgies of the modern theatre have sought to distinguish between 'entertainment' and 'art' in theatre, defined by how each establishes a very different relationship with the audience.

Modernism

With the advent of technological modernity in the late nineteenth century, the human agent was displaced, both physically and psychically – whether speaking of the factory worker caught up in mass mechanization (so effectively satirized by Charlie Chaplin in his film *Modern Times*, 1936) or the depersonalizing camera eye of the new medium of film. This depersonalization is at the core of the rise of industrial capitalism, and Modernism sought to give it expression in art. Central to Modernism is the idea of an escape from the degrading imprisonment of the body through elevating art to a timeless, depersonalized, objective status, one entirely autonomous from its social context and divorced from morality (Marjorie Perloff, 'Modernist Studies', 1992, p. 158). In this, the autonomy of the artwork (i.e. its complete distinctiveness from its environment and context) offers resistance to capitalism, where everything has to be transactable, that is, *for* something else.

In a 1967 essay that is foundational to many arguments in theatre and performance studies, art critic Michael Fried specifically names the acknowledgement of an audience 'theatricality', claiming that:

> The success, even the survival, of the arts has come increasingly to depend on their ability to defeat theatre. For theatre has an audience – *it exists for one – in a way other arts do not*; in fact, this more than anything else is what modernist sensibility finds intolerable in theatre generally. (p. 163)

Implicit in Fried's argument is the notion that the artwork's 'awareness' of being spectated embarrassingly lays bare the relationship of service between the product and the consumer of that product. That is, the artwork is only 'art' if the social relations that brought it into being are denied.

Ignoring the audience

The solution offered by the modern theatre to Modernism's desire for a decisive separation of artwork and audience is something apparently quite simple: ignoring the audience. Ignoring the audience avoids the awkward problem of the reciprocity between actor and audience that exposes art's 'autonomy' as a fiction. The idea of a 'fourth wall' separating audiences from the bourgeois rooms of nineteenth-century drama was already an established theatre convention but in Modernism the separation is elevated to the condition of a work being able to lay a claim to being 'art'. French theorist Roland Barthes identifies acting style as key to maintaining this division, writing that the actor 'must not show that he [*sic*] knows how to act well. The actor must prove that he is not enslaved to the spectator (bogged down in "reality", in "humanity")' ('Diderot, Brecht, Eisenstein' in *Image-Music-Text*, 1977, pp. 74–5). That is, the actor must not attend to the presence of an audience but only to their part in producing the representation. Barthes further writes:

> The theatre is precisely that practice which calculates the place of things as they are observed: if I set the spectacle here, the spectator will see this; if I put it elsewhere, he [*sic*] will not, and I can avail myself of this masking effect and play on the illusion it provides. [. . .] There will still be

representation for so long as a subject (author, reader, spectator or voyeur) casts his gaze towards a horizon on which he cuts out the base of a triangle, his eye (or his mind) forming the apex. (p. 69)

It is noticeable that Barthes' geometric frame is a structure of attention in which the spectator's visual focus actively screens out anything in peripheral vision – that is, other audience members sitting around you. Anything that might be described as social is denied or presented as external to the singular relationship between the beholder and the artwork. By association, any indication of audience presence is a disruption. This directly contrasts with dramaturgies of entertainment, which encourage audiences to recognize their presence in the theatre as mattering to the performance (whether through applause, laughter or other vocalizations of appreciation).

Autonomy and absorption

Strindberg's 'Preface' to *Miss Julie* (1888) is often taken as a manifesto for theatrical Naturalism, due to its focus on the interactions of three characters bound by social expectations and presented as unfolding over a near-continuous time period in the kitchen of Miss Julie's house. Naturalism was a movement in the late nineteenth century that sought to present 'real life' on stage, with plausible, ordinary characters (rather than types) undertaking believable actions within real time. There is an apparent contradiction between naturalistic acting and Modernism, for Modernism rejects Naturalism as overly focused on the human or 'nature'. However, Strindberg's Naturalism prefigures Modernism because it springs from a frustration with artificial stage business: that is, theatricality. What Strindberg's 'Naturalism' does is diminish the features of theatre that to his mind distract audiences from absorption in the artwork. The dramaturgy of *Miss Julie* is thus developed on the principle that the play's structure will focus the audiences' attention on the work rather than on the social space of the theatre. In an innovative move for the time, Strindberg eliminates act divisions:

> I have done this because it seems to me that our declining sensibility to illusion would possibly be disturbed by intervals, during which the spectator has time to reflect and thereby escape from the suggestive influence of the dramatist-hypnotist. ('Preface' to *Miss Julie* (1888), 1998, p. 64)

Strindberg's complaints about the relationship between actors and audiences all revolve around the theatre as a social space:

> If we could dispense with the visible orchestra with its distracting lights and faces turned towards the audience; [. . .] if we could get rid of the private proscenium boxes with their giggling

> drinkers and diners; if we could have complete
> darkness in the auditorium. (1888, pp. 68–9)

Once these conditions are in place, the audience no longer
feel present 'socially' – the theatre performance is apparently
separate and autonomous. In Strindberg's formulation,
Naturalism is primarily a strategy to enable the artwork to
deny all social relation to the audience.

A different dramaturgical strategy for a modernist
separation of artwork and audience can be found in the work
of American modernist Gertrude Stein. While a reader can
fit the rhythms of a novel to their personal reading rhythm,
the time of the theatre is pre-given. In her essay 'Plays', Stein
suggests that this leads to the emotion of the audience being
'always either behind or ahead of the play at which you are
looking and to which you are listening. So, your emotion as
an audience member is never going on at the same time as
the action of the play' (1935, p. 58).

Being reminded in this way of our presence in the theatre
brings us back to the social present, distracting us from
private aesthetic experience. Stein's response was to develop
a dramaturgical structure that she described as 'landscape',
focusing on juxtaposition of images and events, rather than a
narrative that unfolds over time:

> I felt that if a play was exactly like a landscape,
> then there would be no difficulty about the
> emotion of the person looking on at the play
> being behind or ahead the play because the

landscape does not have to make acquaintance.
You may have to make acquaintance with it, but
it does not with you. (p. 75)

Stein's plays often expose the conventions and structures of
playwriting – stage directions and direct speech are often
indistinguishable, with the effect that every aspect of the
writing becomes significant in the consideration of the
dramaturgy: even how it is arranged on the page functions
as a form of tacit stage direction in itself.

Legacies of Modernism

What I am calling dramaturgies of autonomy perhaps reached
its most decisive expression in the plays of Samuel Beckett,
whose play *Waiting for Godot* (1953) became notorious as a
play in which nothing happens: that is, even the attention-
holding mechanisms of plot and narrative were denied to
audiences. Beckett's stage directions deliberately avoid
any acknowledgement of an audience's presence by using
architectural reference to the 'auditorium' rather than the
social reference of 'audience':

> *Estragon moves to centre, halts with his back to*
> *auditorium.*
> **Estragon**   Charming spot. (*He turns, advances to*
> *front, halts facing auditorium.*) Inspiring prospects.
> (*He turns to Vladimir.*) Let's go.
> **Vladimir**   All the same . . . that tree . . . (*Turning*
> *towards the auditorium*) . . . that bog. (p. 69)

By the very mechanism of denying co-presence, the features that apparently play to the audience in the here-and-now offer a yet more emphatic denial. The characters appear to invite audience response and yet deny the audience the satisfaction of that response being acknowledged.

In twenty-first-century theatre, director Katie Mitchell uses Stanislavskian rehearsal techniques, in order to direct actors' attention towards complete absorption in their roles, away from attention to the audience (Mitchell, *The Director's Craft*, 2008). It is a directing method that produces theatre works of forensically detailed, geometric and rhythmic beauty that deny any co-presence between audience and performance. In Mitchell's 2014 production of Chekhov's *The Cherry Orchard* (1904) at the Young Vic, she reversed the spatial structure indicated in the play's stage directions, to imply the eponymous cherry orchard was positioned out front (where the audience were sitting). It was uncanny to sit in an auditorium full of people while characters looked out at the audience as though looking at a thicket of trees – doubly denying audience presence, not only by ignoring it but by casting it as something and somewhere else.

In the second half of the twentieth century, these modernist principles of art underlay many practitioners' antagonism towards dramaturgies of entertainment – including the well-made plays of Terence Rattigan and Noël Coward, musicals and other popular forms. The Royal Court's founder George Devine commented that 'the Royal Court ideal is to be likened to an art gallery or a literary magazine' (Rebellato, *1956 and All That*, 1999, p. 113). In other words, theatre could only lay claim to being an art form when it denied the very element that distinguishes it from other art forms – the presence of, and the interaction with, an audience. The elevation of dramaturgies of autonomy, in opposition to dramaturgies of entertainment, also has a class basis: historians have demonstrated how changing behavioural codes for audience behaviour in the twentieth century corresponded with a shift in the class base of theatre-going audiences from working class to middle class (see also David Wiles, *A Short History of Western Performance Space*, 2003; Simon Shepherd and Peter Womack, *English Drama: A Cultural History*, 1996).

In 1950s London, the British Drama League even held lectures, given by leading theatre practitioners, on teaching audiences how to behave. Audiences were encouraged to remain silent; coughing and commentary were seen as disruptions, not part of the fun (Rebellato, 1999, p. 108). The sociability of sitting in an auditorium is thus bracketed out: sitting silent in the dark watching a live representation unfold (whether realist or not) as though there were no audience present has become the unspoken norm from which all other forms of theatre now must differentiate themselves. Yet this norm turns out to have been itself carefully constructed – to the point of having to teach the mid-twentieth century audience how to obey its rules. Further, the establishment of artistic autonomy also diminishes the role of the audience. Rebellato describes this as a shift away from the audience as 'patrons' – that is, being the judges of taste and value, and ultimately the success of the work. Instead, they must sit in reverent silence before the artwork. Audiences are thereby placed in the position of 'clients': the theatre practitioners are the professionals, and it is their right to determine what constitutes excellence (p. 111).

At the Royal Court, the aesthetic produced by this diminishing of the audiences' role in theatrical reception produced some of the most extraordinary plays and productions of the 1950s and 1960s – and with it, secured a place in the middle-class theatre for working-class (largely male) voices (e.g. John Osborne, Arnold Wesker, Harold Pinter, Edward Bond), expanding the territory of what was considered suitable subject matter for the stage. Within this structural arrangement of attention, released from playing to the pre-established tastes of its audience, a variety of performance forms flourished, displaying the influence of surrealism and absurdism. The decisive separation of the artwork from its viewers thus represented a triumph of Modernism in theatrical form, perhaps best epitomized in the pride taken in the way that Samuel Beckett's *Waiting for Godot* (1953) emptied the Arts Theatre in the West End at its first performances. There was, however, a class basis to diminishing the role an audience had in deciding the value of the work, indicating the condescending side of championing the artist's 'right to fail' – a Modernism-influenced exclusion of the audience who 'doesn't get it'.

A comforting convention?

Nicholas Ridout suggests that the experience of the theatre of Western industrial modernity is fundamentally characterized by the unequal relation between audience and spectator: 'It is a theatre in which one group of people spend leisure time sitting in the dark to watch others spend their working time under lights pretending to be other people' (*Stage Fright*, 2006, p. 6). The modernist projection of an unbridgeable divide between audience and performance attempts to overcome this unequal relation by insisting that the artwork is autonomous from its audience. However, it has become a comforting convention, allowing audiences to avoid awkward questions about how the politics of any given work relate to the social structure of its performance. When jolted into recognition of co-presence, Ridout suggests, we become subject to an 'ontological queasiness' (p. 2), a phrase he borrows from Jonas Barish (1981) – we don't know who we are meant to be, being there. Are we ourselves or playing the role of some kind of imagined 'spectator'? Does our absence from the world of the play reconstitute us as voyeurs? While a significant number of contemporary plays presume an uncomplicated (non)relationship with its audiences, some deliberately use our squeamishness about these ambiguities about who we are in the space to achieve their aesthetic.

Sarah Kane's own production of her play *Phaedra's Love* (May 1996) at the Gate Theatre in Notting Hill used this placing of the audience to intensify a sense of voyeurism that transmuted into an accusation of violent complicity. Sat 'on blocks' all around the space, within the living room setting of the play, the spectators were disconcertingly present to one another while invisible to the characters: '[Hippolytus] was whizzing a car, a toy car all around the audience' (unpublished interview with David Farr, artistic director of the Gate, 1996–8). The situation later segued into the audience being 'cast' as members of a savage and revenge-hungry crowd:

> *Theseus pulls Strophe away from Woman 2*
> *who she is attacking.*
> *He rapes her.*
> *The crowd watch and cheer.*
> *When Theseus has finished he cuts her throat.*

> Strophe Theseus.
> Hippolytus.
> Innocent.
> Mother.
> Oh, Mother.

> *She dies.*
> *Man 1 pulls down Hippolytus' trousers.*
> *Woman 2 cuts off his genitals.*
> *They are thrown onto the barbecue.*
> *The children cheer.* (p. 101)

The space was thus deliberately used to place an audience in a specific, and unflattering, relationship to the world of the play. Critics and some audience members found the culminating image of the production, the barbecuing of genitals, laughable in the intimate context (Alex Sierz, *In-Yer-Face Theatre*, 2001, p. 108), inadvertently indicating the power of Kane's gesture. It was precisely the awkwardness of not knowing who 'we' are meant to be as audience, sitting up far too close to the 'representation', that drove the horror of the play. It was not a failure of representation, but rather constitutive of the dramaturgy of the production that the audience should be caught between self and other, between rejecting the representation through laughter and accepting a complicity in the cruelty through their presence as an only semi-fictional voyeuristic crowd. What looked to some like the failure of a modernist divide between audience and actors was in fact a political gesture, of deliberate dramaturgical proximity.

Dramaturgies of the political

Due to its role in structuring attention, dramaturgy always has a politics – even if that politics is to insist that the artwork is autonomous, timeless and without context – that is, apolitical. Equally, being designed to please entails that dramaturgies of entertainment tend to reinforce the social status quo. There is, however, a third dramaturgical mode of audience relation – neither autonomous nor 'for' its audience in the sense of designed to 'serve' it, but rather one that is 'for' the audience in order to challenge and change beliefs and actions in the social world beyond the theatre. An important component of the political is that it may unsettle, provoke or even divide audiences. There are many kinds of dramaturgy that express a political intention – but what they have in common is that they ask audiences to pay attention not only to the events unfolding on stage but also to the wider social context of the ideas and situations represented.

Naturalism

The terms 'Naturalism' and 'realism' in theatre involve mimetic performance, designed to imply a representation of the 'real world', a representation that is as malleable as the philosophical trends that determine what the 'real' constitutes: what counts as theatrically 'natural' in one era may seem distinctly contrived in another. Few playwrights considered to belong to the movement of late nineteenth-century Naturalism, such as Henrik Ibsen, Anton Chekhov and George Bernard Shaw, would today be perceived as offering 'real-life' tableaux. However, the movement's aim to reveal real social conditions was directly political because it sought to critique how social structures shaped peoples' lives. The French novelist and playwright Emile Zola, a leading proponent of 'slice-of-life' drama, said in 1881: 'The psychological man in our modern works is asking more and more compellingly to be determined by his setting, by the environment that produced him' ('Naturalism in the Theatre', p. 370).

Gerhard Hauptmann's Naturalist play *The Weavers* (1893) is one of the earliest examples of political Naturalism. The play was based on real events: Hauptmann's grandfather had been a weaver in the Silesian mountains, where in 1844 the starving weavers, subjected to harsh conditions by the factory owners, and in fear of the new machines that might destroy their livelihood, rose up against their masters. The rebellion was quickly crushed by military intervention.

What is distinctive about the play's dramaturgy is that among the forty or so characters, there is no focus on a single hero or villain. Many of the events of the play are produced through entrances and exits, as new information is brought to the stage or characters rush off to try to save themselves or their situation. The force of the dramaturgy thus functions through the delineation of a social landscape; what is represented is the conflict between one class and another, rather than between individuals.

The British playwright George Bernard Shaw, by contrast, sought to reveal class oppression through focusing on the class whose actions cause the oppression. For example, in *Mrs Warren's Profession* (1904), he examines the cost of sexual and financial double standards, aiming to expose the hypocrisy of middle-class life, which profited from exploitative practices while vocally condemning them. For Shaw, what was key to the play's political force was its dramaturgical form, which he described as a dramaturgy of 'discussion':

> Formerly you had in what was called a well-made play an exposition in the first act, a situation in the second, an unravelling in the third. Now you have exposition, situation and discussion; and the discussion is the test of the playwright. [. . .] The discussion conquered Europe in Ibsen's Doll's House. (*The Quintessence of Ibsenism*, 1928, p. 213)

Shaw suggests that the final scene of Ibsen's *A Doll's House* (1879) delivered a profound dramaturgical shock because having conformed more or less to the entertainment conventions of the well-made play for the most part:

> 'Just at that point in the last act *[where audiences expect reconciliation]* the heroine very unexpectedly stops her emotional acting and says: "We must sit down and discuss all this that has been happening between us"' (p. 219).

Ibsen's stage directions indeed suggest a change in the temperature of emotions depicted on stage. Nora's tone shifts to a register that mirrors her sense of being 'calm and collected':

> **Nora**   Papa used to call me his baby doll, and he played with me as I used to play with my dolls. Then I came to live in your house . . .
>
> **Helmer**   What way is that to talk about our marriage?
>
> **Nora** (*imperturbably*)   What I mean is: I passed out of Daddy's hands into yours. You arranged everything to your tastes, and I acquired the same tastes.
>
> (Act 3, p. 80)

It is telling that Nora's alteration in tone, shifting from drama to discussion, is rarely marked, even in productions of the play today – indicating the way that the movement of Naturalism has lost much of its political force. As director John McGrath pointed out in *A Good Night Out* (1981), the political efficacy of staged revelations of social injustice is questionable when the question of what kind of audience it is 'for' is not taken into account. Is to reveal social conditions enough? When does the telling of a previously unvoiced story become tainted by a prurient politics of display? McGrath says of the Royal Court's post-war programme of plays about working-class life:

> This famed New Era/Dawn/Direction of British theatre was no more than the elaboration of a theatrical technique for turning authentic working-class experience into satisfying thrills for the bourgeoisie. (p. 11)

Where the social context depicted does not mirror the context of its reception, such dramaturgies of Naturalism can have the effect of confirming rather than puncturing the status quo – the 'unequal' status of at-leisure theatregoers and the working actors makes the representation of the experience of one class, when presented to another class, re-establish rather than upend the norms of structural class inequality, especially when the majority of the people involved in staging plays about working class life are themselves middle class.

The epic theatre

The immensely influential early-twentieth-century German director and playwright Bertolt Brecht decisively rejected Naturalism as a mode of creating political theatre – it might be 'for' an audience in the sense of revealing the real conditions of an oppressed class, but it also had the unfortunate effect of casting the audience as passive recipients of that revelation, rather than developing the capacity of the audience to act for social change – which for Brecht was a condition of the political theatre.

Brecht's anti-capitalist theories of the epic theatre offer probably the most famous – and influential – form of political dramaturgy in Western industrial modernity. Not only did Brecht develop dramaturgical precepts for enabling audiences to engage politically, he also demonstrated how the 'dramatic' theatre (against which he defines the 'epic' theatre) works to maintain the status quo. Brecht evolved his theories of theatre through writing and directing his plays in Berlin in the 1920s and 1930s, and then across Europe when exiled from Germany by Hitler's Nazi government. After the war Brecht returned to East Germany, due to his lifelong socialism ('socialism' is an umbrella term for political and economic systems that seek to distribute wealth and rights equitably).

Brecht describes the dramatic theatre as orientated to 'feelings', 'immersion', seeing human nature as 'fixed' and 'unchangeable', with each scene developing towards the next in a linear structure of events (*Brecht on Theatre*, 2015, p. 65). What concerns Brecht is how dramatic structure is used to encourage audiences to speculate on the interior life of the characters – to project individuality onto the representation – and to become absorbed in what might happen next, without thought for wider social implications. Brecht's list of what constitutes 'dramatic' theatre reveals 'absorption' not as a condition of the experience of art but rather as suggesting a given natural order – 'how things are' – that then invites people to resign themselves to the status quo (p. 65). This dramaturgy is contrasted with the 'epic' theatre, which 'turns spectators into observers' by turning emotions into insights, proceeding by montage, 'each scene for itself'. These are all techniques designed to make humans an 'object of investigation', representing 'human nature as a process'. In the epic theatre, 'social being determines thought'. Central to the epic theatre is the idea of distanciation (also known as the 'alienation effect'), to demonstrate that the social world is constructed rather than natural and – vitally – that therefore people can change it.

One dramaturgical technique that Brecht uses is the episodic form – the idea of 'each scene for itself' (p. 65) – to provide breaks in dramatic action, in order to disrupt absorption in character and draw audiences' attention to the situation instead. For example, the final scene of *Mother Courage* (1941) breaks with conventional dramaturgical expectations of narrative. In the penultimate scene, Kattrin, Mother Courage's disabled daughter and the last of her children still living, is shot dead for heroically alerting the town to the arrival of the invading army. Instead of being a scene of mourning, the final scene does not acknowledge the apparent dramatic climax of the previous scene. Instead it merely depicts Mother Courage on the road again, her final words being: 'Got to get back in business again' (p. 186). As a depiction of how people are conditioned by circumstance, the juxtaposition of Kattrin's heroic death with her mother's pragmatism makes the pain of loss feel all the more acute. We mourn Kattrin as spectators partly because we can see how her mother cannot afford to – exemplifying Brecht's maxim 'social being determines thought' (*Brecht on Theatre*, p. 65).

Brecht's legacy

Most left-wing British playwrights of the later twentieth century owe something to the Brechtian idea of the epic in their political work 'for' audiences, including Caryl Churchill, David Hare, Edward Bond, Joan Littlewood, Tony Kushner, John Arden and David Edgar. Caryl Churchill's *Serious Money* (1987) satirizes the culture of greed-as-value at the level of dramaturgy. Written through a collective process in 1987, at the height of the power of Margaret Thatcher, the British prime minister who introduced neoliberal capitalism to Britain, *Serious Money* satirizes financial culture in fast-paced verse that is as pleasurable as it is defamiliarizing. The play offers a savage satirical indictment of the City – London's financial heart – and the burgeoning Thatcherite financial culture in which everything is costed and nothing valued. Dramaturgically, its epic structure continuously destabilizes any alignment of values between character and action, particularly with regard to Stella, a central character. She starts the play determined to uncover the cause of her stockbroker brother Jake's death, but in a slippage barely noticed – tellingly – even by the audience, ends up going after the money instead. The genre of detective thriller is maintained but the object shifts; and in performing this sleight of hand, Churchill delineates how easy it is to become distracted from what really matters. In this, Churchill indicts a whole society.

Get out of the theatre (and into performance)

Another way of thinking about how dramaturgy works politically is to explore its relationship to places of performance and therefore the architecture of theatres. Precisely because political theatre is concerned with its context, the changing landscape of social and political expression in theatre brings together the architectural dramaturgy of buildings with the dramaturgies of plays and productions. In Britain after the end of the Second World War, the Arts Council was founded to create a new subsidized sector to support, specifically, the development of British art. Across the UK, civic theatres were built in towns and cities to house productions of plays. Architecturally, these theatres were intended to be 'democratic' in terms of allowing every audience member a similar, and unobstructed, view of the stage (Northern Stage in Newcastle is an example of one such theatre). However, it quickly became apparent that these theatres in fact perpetuated class divides through being created by, and for, the urban and suburban, often university-educated, middle classes. Far from inviting everyone into the theatre, this architecture was most suited to the presentation of what I have described as dramaturgies of autonomy. Separation from the art was privileged through the architecture of the end-on space and designed to offer the least possible social intrusion on the presentation of the drama. This was alienating for working-class performance traditions that – from music hall to circus, to pantomime – actively courted vocal audience response.

In resistance to this formalization of theatre, Britain saw a proliferation of theatre that took place outside theatres. Getting out of the theatre was motivated not by the aesthetic interests that today generally govern what is often called site-specific theatre, or even theatre on the fringe. The aim was rather a desire to connect directly with audiences who felt excluded from theatre buildings – as Baz Kershaw describes in *The Politics of Performance* (1992):

> A theatre building is not so much the empty space of the creative artist, nor a democratic institution of free speech, but rather a kind of social engine that helps to drive an unfair system of privilege. The theatre achieves this through ensnaring every kind of audience in a web of mostly unacknowledged values, tacit commitments to forces that are beyond their control, and mechanisms of exclusion that ensure most people stay away. Hence, performances in theatre buildings are deeply embedded in theatre as a *disciplinary system*. (p. 31)

Kershaw's argument exposes again how the notion of 'losing' yourself in contemplation of the work tends to assume a particular type of person doing the looking. Should you be excluded from the class, gender or ethnic assumptions of the work, it is much harder to become absorbed. In reaction against theatre's tacit and explicit denials of the diversity – in class, gender, sexuality and ethnicity – of the British post-war population, many practitioners in the 1960s, 1970s and 1980s started their own theatre companies, specifically set up to redress the imbalance – including, perhaps most famously, but by no means limited to Temba (1972–92), Black Mime (1987–98), Talawa (1985–present), the Black Theatre Co-operative (now called nitroBEAT, 1979–present), the Black Theatre

Forum (1985–2001), Monstrous Regiment (1975–93), The Women's Theatre Group (1973–90, now Sphinx Theatre Company 1991–present) and Gay Sweatshop (1974–97).

What unites the experimental dramaturgies of the productions by such companies – which moved from spectacle to direct address, to film montage, to entertainment, to dramatic absorption, often in the same performance – is how they were conceived with specific audiences in mind. As a result, many performance works were produced outside established theatres, offering a different dramaturgy in the very architecture of the event. These drew on a rich twentieth-century history of using non-theatrical spaces across Europe and, later, the United States. For example, inspired by Soviet 'agitprop' theatre (merging 'agitation' and 'propaganda'), which sought to educate people about communism in early-twentieth-century Russia, the 1930s UK Workers' Theatre Movement created a network of locally active British theatre groups, which staged street theatre that dealt with social inequality – aiming to awaken recognition in their working-class, often factory-employed, audiences of their repression by the capitalist system and to encourage them to join the class struggle:

> We have to go there where the masses are: in meetings, in workers' affairs, on the streets, at factory gates, to parades, at picnics, in working-class neighbourhoods. That means we must be mobile. (Red Stage: Organ of the Workers' Theatre, pamphlet (February 1932), 1)

Similarly in the United States, as part of the Roosevelt New Deal in response to the Great Depression of the 1930s, the Federal Theatre Project developed 'Living Newspapers', which presented topical social issues in performance form before being shut down by the very government that had initially funded them (Rania Karoula, *The Federal Theatre Project 1935–1939*, 2020).

Further, across the twentieth century and beyond, repelled by – as well as excluded from – the (male) traditions of theatre production, feminist performers and theatre makers, like many other politicized groups with socially marginalized and culturally under-represented identities, have exited the formal spaces of theatre in wave after wave. Beyond theatre buildings, many have invented dramaturgies of performance to enable artistic expression to flourish, on the basis that in French feminist Hélène Cixous' words: 'if you don't write, someone else will write you' (April de Angelis, Doctoral Thesis: *Interrogating a New Feminist Dramaturgy*, 2013, p. 6). Nevertheless, this 'writing' was not a masculine mode of textual monument-building – so much so, that often there are few documents of the performances created – making it much harder to reconstruct the dramaturgical work of alternative performance groups than it is with plays that are published as well as performed. As playwright April de Angelis says of her involvement with Resisters in the 1980s, a theatre collective of global majority and white women whose purpose was 'the placing of women centre-stage in order to relate and examine in a political context the hidden experiences of women such as domestic violence', the plays were 'ephemeral, never published' (p. 4).

Indeed, female artists in the visual arts have been drawn to performance precisely because of the sense that the ephemeral nature of live presence held a promise of evading pre-written structures of coercion. Reflecting on this history, feminist theatre theorist Peggy Phelan famously argued in the early 1990s: 'Performance's being [. . .] becomes itself through disappearance', and in doing so evades outside control: 'Performance cannot be saved, recorded, documented or otherwise participate in the circulation of representations of representations' (*Unmarked: the Politics of Performance*, 1993, p. 146). A rich strand of solo feminist performance art emerged from the 1960s onwards, in which a turn to the body as a primary site of meaning was authenticated through collapsing the roles of creator and performer. From Carolee Schneemann to Marina Abramovic, the work of a wide range of artists who came to prominence in the 1960s and 1970s was influential in the later development of live art as a category of performance-making – one which rejects dramaturgies that separate the real and representational.

Equally, the careers of many feminist performers and playwrights were forged in the collaborative practices of theatre companies that sought to upend the established order; they did so not only in the content of the work but also through the process by which it was made. Importantly, often the works would be devised by the company or multiply-authored, such that the notions of collectivity and egalitarianism that shaped the relationship between these forms of theatre with their audiences also shaped the working relations between theatre makers. In doing so, practitioners carved out a space for art by marginalized identities that did not conform to – or require – (white) patriarchal determinations of what constitutes art and the artist. In other words, the idea of the individual artist-genius enshrined in Modernism – Strindberg's 'dramatist-hypnotist' (*Preface*, p. 64) – was under attack.

Dramaturgies of participation

With proliferating media for the promulgation of political messages in the contemporary world, what place does performance have today in articulating social questions? In the 1990s, art critic Nicolas Bourriaud unleashed a new wave of conversation with regard to the relationship between the artwork and audiences in his book *Relational Aesthetics* (2002/1998), which laid claim to the practising of social relations *as* art. Bourriaud links this to the advent and ever-increasing encroachment of digital technologies in modern life on our capacity to engage with others in everyday life:

> The general mechanisation of social functions gradually reduces the relational space [. . .] Professional behaviour patterns are modelled on the efficiency of the machines replacing them, these machines carrying out tasks which once represented so many opportunities for exchanges, pleasure and squabbling. (p. 17)

He goes on to claim that 'Contemporary art is definitely developing a political project when it endeavours to move into the relational realm' (p. 17). On this argument, any act of people coming together – whether for a meal or to have a conversation – could be staged as an artwork, representing the relational qualities of mutual engagement, as a resistance against alienation in modern societies. However, as critics of Bourriaud have pointed out, making social interactions part of the dramaturgical structure of the artwork does not automatically make it political, for it depends entirely on how the audience are positioned in relation to the purpose of the work (Claire Bishop, 'Antagonism and Relational Aesthetics', 2004, pp. 51–79).

A plethora of forms

Over the past fifteen years, performance works that directly involve the audience in the work (through movement, interaction, decision-making, conversation, digital engagement and so on) have become commonplace. Often these kinds of theatre are discussed primarily in terms of how they contrast with the kinds of dramaturgy encoded in plays written to be performed for an audience who do not directly affect how the representation unfolds. In this, popular discourse conforms to the opposition between 'active' and 'passive' spectatorship critiqued by the philosopher Jacques Rancière (*The Emancipated Spectator*, 2008). Only a little pressure on these terms breaks down the supposed binary between 'active' and 'passive', or 'acting' and 'viewing' (Rancière, 2008, pp. 11–13). Indeed, it is not clear that sitting in a darkened auditorium watching a show involves passivity, when emotional experience is taken into account (fascinatingly, a 2017 University College London study found that watching a live theatre performance can stimulate the heart to the same extent as twenty-eight minutes of physical exercise). Similarly, many have questioned the idea that interacting with the performance makes an audience 'active'.

In this context, director and maker Tassos Stevens, who runs Coney, a game-making, change-inspiring performance company, finds it frustrating that very different kinds of interactive dramaturgies are often bracketed together in the media, when in reality there is as much variety in dramaturgical form and impact across work that is variously described as 'immersive', 'participatory', 'site-specific' or 'site-responsive' as there is in more 'traditional' dramaturgies. This is reflected in the expansion of the scholarly field in this area, as exemplified, for example, in Trencsényi and Cochrane's *New Dramaturgy* (2014), *Performing Proximity* (2014) by Leslie Hill and Helen Paris and Josephine Machon's *Immersive Theatres* (2013). Like traditional dramaturgies, interactive works can be differentiated through how they establish their relationship with their audience. Thus the 'immersive experience' of commercial performance events are clearly dramaturgies of entertainment, designed to serve – and delight – their audiences. Examples include the City of London's *The War of the Worlds* (2022) and, since 2007, Secret Cinema's spectacular recreations of popular films, which invite audience members 'to become part of the story yourself', as it declares on its website (accessed 2022). Meanwhile, the participatory spectacles of British performance company Punchdrunk could be said to emerge from the principles of the dramaturgy of autonomy: masked audiences are encouraged to wander around hugely detailed scenic spaces, created in warehouses or other found spaces, where they may or may not happen upon events significant to a central narrative while discovering a plethora of thematically resonant subplots. Although there is occasional direct interaction with audiences, the performance is clearly independent of them.

Participation and politics

Although the emancipatory potential of claims about the agency and sociability of dramaturgical forms that place audiences in the position of interacting with the work is undoubtedly overstated, participatory dramaturgies can also take political form. Part of the politics of the dramaturgy of *World Factory* (2013–17), an interactive performance produced by the Young Vic, London, and New Wolsey, Ipswich, that I co-directed with artist Simon Daw, involved delving into the lack of agency most people have, globally, under conditions of consumer capitalism. At the heart of the show was a scenario-based card game, with multiple routes and outcomes, interlinking questions of ethics, fashion, environmental impacts, working conditions, migration and globalization. Audience members sat round small tables in groups of six and were invited to make decisions about how to run a small clothing factory in China. A 'dealer' (performer) would deal a card that on the front described a situation and on the back, two opposing options for how to respond. Based on extensive research, the game structure thus mimicked the lack of real-world alternatives available to those caught up in the system. Each small group was invited to make a decision together (but not directed how to do so), which they would convey to the 'dealer' using a shop scanner to 'bleep' a barcode on the card (*World Factory: The Game*, 2017). Casino-style, audiences traded in workers and money – but it was a game in which the audience had to decide what it means to 'win'.

The political dramaturgy of *World Factory* emerged from the desire to reposition the audiences' relationship to the representation, away from dramaturgies that privilege individual psychology and invite audiences to judge others' behaviours. Immersing audiences in the complexity of ethical decision-making was a provocation to audience members to consider their own position in the system. In this lay its politics, as it confronted audiences with a world in which ethics and actions were rarely consistent. An alliance between theatre etiquette and the presumption (not stated) of competition organized by the game meant that the desire to survive within the system of consumer capitalism often led to decisions that took audiences on what they later considered to be unethical routes, regardless of their professed intentions.

Yet the politics of the work also depended not on any given decision by any given audience member but on the utopian energy of the collaborations (and conflicts) between audience members in the context of playing the game. Yes, the situation thus delineated could be called dystopian, if it weren't demonstrably based on several years of research into the history and conditions of the clothing industry in China and the UK (*World Factory: The Game*, 2017). But due to the lively, engaged and wide-ranging conversations among audiences, there remained (I hope) a more utopian implication that it is by coming together in these relational ways that we can start to address the alienating effect of the all-pervasiveness of the techno-capitalist system described by Bourriaud.

What participatory dramaturgies arguably can do particularly well is draw greater attention to the structures of power that govern both the theatre event and the situation that the event is representing – in particular where audience members are asked to make decisions that alter the event in some way. This is largely due to such dramaturgies often being slightly less familiar to their audiences, so they are likely to be more alert to how the work has been constructed. However, what I hope to have shown in Part 1 is how the politics of a work of theatre is dependent not only on subject matter but also on the context – social and architectural – in which the performance takes place. Dramaturgy is significant in this, because the politics of the work lies as much in its form as in its content – not so much in what characters say, however political their statements, but in the dramaturgical relations (including with an audience) that structure the work overall. Further, while sitting in silence, absorbed in the representation unfolding in front of you, became synonymous in the twentieth century with what theatre *is*, I hope to have defamiliarized it sufficiently for you to regard it as just one form of theatre among many.

2 dramaturgy and power

In this part I take a different approach to dramaturgy, to unpick its relationship to wider structures of power beyond the theatre, which are often consciously – or unconsciously – reflected back in the dramaturgical structure of theatre performances. I look at how dramaturgies reflect their social context in ways that are either deliberate and declared by the work or are tacit, unconsciously replicating and reflecting the inequities of the wider culture.

Dramaturgy and economy

On the face of it, economics and dramaturgy seem worlds apart. But economics, like dramaturgy, shapes how people understand their relationships to one another. Like dramaturgy, it is a slippery term, because it names the arrangement of relations, rather than a 'thing' in itself. What also – crucially – links dramaturgy and economics is the way each tacitly constructs notions of who we are.

While dramaturgy self-evidently relates to representations of reality, rather than reality itself, economics purports to represent facts. However, economics is also a cultural system, and contemporary economics in Western culture relies on a story about human nature that reduces its complexities to a predictable narrative: that a human will, given the chance, behave selfishly. Economist Kate Raworth describes this figure as a man 'standing alone, money in hand, calculator in head, and ego in heart', and – significantly – with nature beneath his feet: 'he has told us that we are self-interested, calculating, fixed in taste, and dominant over nature' (*Doughnut Economics: Seven Ways to Think Like a 21st-Century Economist,* 2017, p. 96/p. 28). What is so powerful about this image, Raworth goes on to show, is that the more people believe that humans are driven only by self-interest, the more likely people are to behave in this way. Thus, the representation of the human in economics, which is essentially a story, has become the presumed basis of reason: 'Rational economic man came to define rationality' (p. 99).

Theatre has danced with the values of capitalism since its earliest incarnation in the 1500s, both as a theme and as a way of understanding humans as independent of their circumstances – and able to act to change them. The essential principles of capitalism involve using money or resources to make more money – through buying or selling goods and services. The idea is that the 'market' will regulate prices – that is, a good or service is only worth what someone will pay for it regardless of how much labour went into it or the quality of resources used. Thus, when an item is scarce or rare, prices go up. When in abundance, prices go down. This view of the economy depends on everyone operating in their own self-interest – for example, getting the cheapest possible price for something, regardless of circumstance. This behaviour is what is described as 'rational' in modern economics, devaluing other kinds of human engagement or motivation, such as striving on behalf of others, not just oneself.

Mirroring the values of the market economy, many dramaturgies in capitalist societies focus on the success – or failure – of individuals and invite us to judge them for their actions. This focus of dramaturgy can be traced back to the febrile culture of early modern England, and particularly London, in which the appropriation of resources from the Americas fostered early capitalism and was creating a new kind of person: one whose wealth and status were not dependent on birth and the unchangeable ties of feudal obligation. Through profiting from the appropriation and destruction of lands and resources across the world with little or no repercussions for Europeans, Europeans of non-aristocratic descent could form their own (self)presentation and standing in the world. The plays of Shakespeare and his contemporaries are full of characters trying (and often failing) to find their way in this new culture, in which the entwined forces of colonialism and capitalism were reshaping all cultural relations.

As a result, the dramaturgies of many plays in the West pattern out a particular idea of what it means to be a successful person within a capitalist society. Shakespeare's characterization of Henry V's reign in his play of that name depicts the character behaving in ways that could be identified as capitalist, indicating a fundamental break with the feudal system. Shakespeare's Henry V, unlike his predecessor kings Richard II and Henry IV, knows what he wants, and right from his appearances in the *Henry IV* parts 1 and 2 onwards he is planning, projecting forward and storing up his considerable personal, financial and social capital towards deploying it when the time is right – and winning. Once Henry wins the hearts and minds of the nation by his planned transformation from rascal to regal, he chooses to lead his country into war – an act of capital accumulation. Once in France, he gathers his information, he works out his plan and strikes at the right time – he capitalizes on the power of rhetoric, and he wins the day, against all the apparent odds, much as a canny stock market speculator might. When it comes to claiming his prize – France – he describes marrying the king of France's daughter as his 'capital demand' (Act 5, scene 2, line 98). *Henry V* is nevertheless a play that is deeply ambivalent about this kind of capitalist 'winning'. Not only does it show the cost of war to the English as well as the French, it depicts Henry as betraying his former friends in order to maintain the hierarchy of control over others.

Dramaturgies of winners and losers

Rapid urbanization, and the emergence of a new professional middle-class in the wake of the industrial revolution, is another point at which capitalism and exploitation stimulated a cultural renaissance in theatre across Europe, from the late nineteenth century onwards. An early example is the aspirational Jean in Strindberg's *Miss Julie* (1888), who plans to exploit the situation of having had sex with his master's daughter by absconding with Miss Julie's money to start his dream hotel. Not much later, the more likeable (but for that, all the more representative of a shift of values) local peasant-turned-wealthy businessman Lopakhin in Chekhov's *The Cherry Orchard* (1904) attempts to stem the tragic trajectory of its impoverished aristocrat owners, by advising them to chop down their cherry tree orchard in order to build holiday homes. At the end of the play, when 'the only thing that can be heard, far away in the orchard, is the thudding of the axe' (p. 67) we know that the 'rational' Lopakhin, representative of the new order, has turned his advice to his own advantage, having bought up his aristocratic neighbours' land after they have been forced to sell it.

Indeed, particularly critical moments in the history of capitalism seem to prove fertile for plays that continue to have resonance today: whether a London society and economy newly fuelled by colonial theft from across the Globe in Shakespeare's time, the rapid urbanization and industrialization of the late nineteenth century across Europe or the emergence of North America's global dominance during and in the wake of the Second World War. At each of these points, capitalism has been visible as a system. Mid-century American playwright Arthur Miller's plays problematize and valorize capitalism through examining the impact of the 'American Dream' – that is, the belief that if you work hard and play your cards right anyone can make it – and that therefore your success is down to you, as an individual. What is represented is a zero-sum game – the winners can only win if the losers lose.

Whether it is Willy Loman's son Biff in Miller's *Death of a Salesman* (1949), who only wants to be accepted for who he is, or Willy himself, who cannot forgive himself for failing to live up to an image that never existed, Miller's dramaturgy invites us to feel empathy for the 'losers' in the system. Yet this empathy also places the audience in a superior position in relation to the characters, through inspiring pity, while the dramaturgy reinforces the values of the capitalist culture that damages them. In Miller's *All My Sons* (1947), Joe Keller is accused by his son Chris of being responsible for causing airmens' deaths by knowingly supplying defective aeroplane parts to the American airforce; he defends himself on the basis that he merely participated in an exploitative system. However, the play's dramaturgy focuses attention on his individual responsibility, rather than inviting recognition of collective culpability for a system that rewards exploitation and duplicity in the name of profit. The narrative promise of political critique is overwhelmed by the absorbing dramaturgy of individual betrayal.

Mid-century American dramatist Tennessee Williams' plays are far more troubled by the masculinist heteronormativity of American bourgeois capitalism than his contemporary Arthur Miller's. Nevertheless, Williams presents Stanley in *A Streetcar Named Desire* (1947) as representative of a new order, whose heteronormative masculinity cannot coexist with his wife's sister Blanche's fragile grip on sanity, maintained only by a patina of class superiority. Blanche's ability to distinguish self and other finally dissolves after Stanley rapes her. The dramaturgy makes it feel inevitable that Blanche's sister Stella, when forced to choose between believing her sister and her husband, the old world and the new, those who are damaged and those who damage, should decide to accept Stanley's narrative over Blanche's – even though the sympathies of the play are decisively with Blanche.

The dramaturgies of these plays, then, ask us to judge the characters who 'win' under capitalism for their behaviour, but at the same time to accept their power. Such plays thus uphold the idea of human self-interest as 'rational' (as claimed by the economic advocates of capitalism), however damaging it is to those who do not fit the narrative. Some plays mourn this state of affairs, while others tacitly celebrate it. All can be seen as either normalizing this narrowly defined story of who we are or as simply reflecting the state of modern capitalism. Just because we are invited in Miller's and Williams' plays to share the pain of those who lose out, it does not mean that what emerges is any other proposition for how to live. Indeed, whether reflecting reality or normalizing an economically determined narrative of power, a dramaturgy that holds the attention of the audience through patterns of winning and losing within capitalist societies 'others' all those whose position in the system does not comfortably permit individual agency. Another way, therefore, of describing what I am calling 'dramaturgies of winners and losers' is as the dramaturgy of capitalism.

Critiquing racial capitalism

Alice Childress' play *Trouble in Mind* (1955) sheds light on such dramaturgies from the perspective of those who are racially othered, directly tackling the relationship between dramaturgy, race and capitalism. Winning an Obie award, and staged to acclaim off Broadway in 1955, *Trouble in Mind* was optioned by producers for transferring to New York's famed commercial theatre sector, Broadway, on condition that Childress rewrite the ending – but when she was not willing to let the white characters off the hook, the production was shelved. In this, life was imitating art, as the play charts the rehearsals for a Broadway production of a racist play about a lynching, which collapses when Wiletta, a senior Black actress, points out the racist dramaturgical structure of the play they are rehearsing: 'the writer wants the damn white man to be the hero – and I'm the villain' (p. 106). The white male director has previously called on the demands of commercial theatre – to please its audience – to justify the play's racial stereotyping: 'We don't want to antagonize the audience' (p. 97). This bears out Wiletta's repeated refrain that 'it's the man's play, the man's money, and the man's theater' (p. 57). Wiletta's courage in articulating the racism of the play they are rehearsing plays out against a backdrop of economic endangerment for the characters, due to their dependence on the very system (of theatre and of society) that excludes their humanity. Yet despite the message of the play, it was precisely this entwinement of capitalist investment, ownership and theatrical dramaturgy that also prevented the actual play in which the character of Wiletta speaks these lines from taking up its rightful place on Broadway.

Childress not only points out the irrationality of the racism; she also resists the crushing of characters that a dramaturgy of winners and losers would require (as happens to Blanche in Williams' *Streetcar*). Instead, the play ends in radical uncertainty and discussion, and finally, with a brief moment of dramaturgical emancipation that is utopian in gesture, when Wiletta takes centre stage. In the fiction, she is performing to an empty auditorium, but in actual performance, in front of a real audience, what it means is that the play ends by centring the perspective of a Black female character, with the actor playing her given the dramaturgically significant task of closing the show. This positioning fulfils one of Wiletta's stated dreams (long thwarted by minor roles involving racist stereotypes), 'to stand forth at my best [. . .] to stand up here and do anything I want' (p. 114). Crucially, it also counters the ingrained white supremacy of the theatre industry (now as then) that rarely offers complex protagonist roles specifically written for Black women. While the ending in the actual theatre celebrates centring Wiletta's story, the empty theatre of the fiction reminds audiences: dismantling racialized (and gender) hierarchies is an ongoing project.

Dramaturgy and marginalization

This section will focus on trying to articulate and denaturalize theatre industry norms, subsumed in the pursuit of 'what works', which can silence important questioning of the dominant logic (much as the director depicted in *Trouble in Mind* passes off his racism as financial pragmatism). It therefore looks at the consequences of how dramaturgy encodes norms of power – and at ways of using dramaturgy to create other models. Dramaturgy is an attention structure designed to highlight what matters to the story – and this shaping of what is foregrounded is what makes it a practice of art. At the same time, this same practice of dramaturgy intersects with the uneven power balances of the society it is produced within, entailing that the structure may merely unintentionally reflect dominant power structures. Therefore, attention to dramaturgical structure is essential for ensuring that the decisions that construct the work are deliberate and reflective of the work's aims. There is a leaning towards discussion of representation of cis women in this section, not only because of my own context, but because they/we form almost 50 per cent of the population. This indicates how the imbalances I am discussing are indicative of an uneven distribution of power among different identities that cannot be excused or dismissed by insistence on a 'majority' perspective in terms of numbers. These imbalances are, of course, further intensified by the intersectional nature of multiple marginalized identities that any one person might embody.

The dramaturgy of *Fairview* (2018), by African American playwright Jackie Sibblies Drury, reveals how theatre etiquette, the socio-aesthetic 'rules' audiences take for granted, allows privileged groups to ignore other equally deep-seated and unspoken rules – in this case, those which render a society racist and entrench power further in the (white) hands of those who already hold it. Over three acts, the racialized space of the theatre is made explicit – as a cipher for, and demonstration of, how white supremacy functions at a dramaturgical level. The play begins naturalistically, centred on an African American middle-class family of a type familiar from television comedy, that reveals itself to be subject to the white gaze – a gaze that increasingly interferes actively in the action – ending with the tables turned on the white viewers who are asked up on stage, to be placed under literal and figurative scrutiny by the global majority audience in the theatre. *Fairview*, like *Trouble in Mind*, deploys dramaturgy to move attention from individual flaws to the structural conditions that are the default lens in white Western society. But unlike Childress' move of creating a conduit of hope, *Fairview* presents rupture but does not make a proposition for repair. White supremacy has been revealed as a constitutive element in classical dramaturgy, without a proposition to move beyond it. That proposition does, however, come in another play by Jackie Sibblies Drury, *Marys Seacole* (2022), through its dramaturgical reconfiguration of heroism away from the image of the white saviour, in the way it refracts the biography of a historical figure across eras, situations and colonial geography to explore how the heavy burden of care falls on global majority women in white supremacist societies. In this, the title 'Marys Seacole' is crucial, that additional 's' at the end of Mary suggesting there is no singular self, separate from the different contexts we find ourselves in.

Unusual as it is for a play to make the very dramaturgy of structural inequity its topic, much work has been done beyond the theatre by anti-racist and intersectionally feminist movements, to expose the uneven distribution of power in relations between people, embedded in the institutions and cultures of Western society. Those in the dominant position in these normalized power structures often express incredulity or anger when they are invited to recognize their embedded advantage. Social theorist David Graeber describes the reaction of some male high school students in North America as outrage or even outright refusal, when set a creative writing exercise whose brief is to imagine yourself transformed into another gender for a day (*Utopia of Rules*, 2015, p. 70). The widespread reluctance to countenance a conversation regarding race-determined structural violence is what led to journalist and author Reni Eddo-Lodge's blog and then book, *Why I'm No Longer Talking to White People about Race* (2017). A source of the disproportionate outrage that is unleashed by calling those in positions of power to account is, as she points out, that 'They've never had to think about what it means, in power terms, to be white, so any time they're vaguely reminded of this fact, they interpret it as an affront' (p. x).

This exposure of people's experience and actions as the product of – and designed by – systems of power acts as a reminder that each of us is the sum of all our past, present and potential power relations. Recognizing this goes against the concept of the self in capitalism as an individual separate from all others. These uneven relations of power are not specific to theatre; what could be described as a 'dramaturgy of power' plays out in a wide variety of environments where people come together to participate in live events that have a prearranged structure – from sports events, to board meetings, to political speeches or academic conferences. What is significant for understanding dramaturgy, however, is that it is in the *form* of the work that relations of power are embedded and exert influence. Works might have a political message while formally reflecting and corroborating the status quo, or the reverse. In addition to the politics that are described in the work, recognizing the role of the dramaturgy of the work helps directors and producers understand the political impact of the way that the structure of the work represents power. What Childress' play *Trouble in Mind* makes clear is that a simplistic policy of 'inclusion' of any person or group with one or more characteristics protected in law, while statistically significant in terms of the distribution of employment, is not enough to transform cultural representation. For dramaturgy itself can either reinforce pre-existing structures of power or can start to work to propose alternatives.

Dramaturgy and representation

How a play opens, as well as how it is resolved, determines how audiences understand what the main aim of the play is. Similarly, a focus on specific characters is also part of the way plays structure the attention of the audience. Dramaturgies that focus on a core character (whether one or a small number) tend to represent only those aspects of other characters that are necessary for the audiences' understanding of that central character. This can be understood, positively, as bringing dramaturgical clarity; plays with a plethora of characters are frequently regarded as unfocused. That said, this interpretation could also be understood as part of a cultural landscape that expects to 'get' something for its money, to be delivered a 'service' and offered an easily digestible message.

In obvious ways, those characters who are more consistently featured in a play-text attract more attention. What is less apparent is the way that, through this process, some characters are rendered oddly absent while present, through being designed only to illuminate the qualities of other characters. This might be said of the character of Ophelia in Shakespeare's *Hamlet* (1609), her function being to illuminate the desires, actions and hypocrisies of her father, brother and lover. The lack of subjectivity in the character is presented in many productions, even today, as a feminine norm. When I worked as dramaturg/co-director on the Globe's 2022 ensemble production, played in the indoor Sam Wanamaker Playhouse our method of handling this lack of intrinsic characterization was to foreground how Ophelia is used by the male characters and is never permitted to speak for herself. Rather than making the popular faux feminist move of making her a little 'feisty', which merely disguises how little the play is interested in her perspective, we sought to reveal the patriarchal and misogynist conditions of the fictional situation that deny her any voice of her own. We were also able to present, therefore, her famous loss of sanity not only as the outcome of grief and rejection but also as a tragic reclaiming of agency. In doing so, her 'mad' scene becomes a moment of insurrection against the forces that would destroy her.

According to a 2012 investigation by theatre director Elizabeth Freestone and The Guardian newspaper, only around one-third of characters in plays in contemporary performance are gendered female, 16 per cent of Shakespeare's characters. This was corroborated by inhouse research I did with the New Wolsey Theatre, Ipswich, 2016–18, as part of Tonic Theatre's 'Advance' programme. This perhaps reflects the ongoing predominance of male directors and writers in theatre, as analysed by Sphinx Theatre in 2019. In most performance seasons in the subsidized and commercial theatre, there are likely to be significantly fewer representations of women on stage than there are women in the general population. Further, many of the female characters are created for the dramaturgical purpose of telling the stories of male protagonists.

What is significant in the dramaturgical focus on men (and predominantly straight white men) is not only that what is deemed of interest to or about people of the global majority, women and/or those of a range of non-normative gender identities is circumscribed. It is also a reflection of the fact that in Western society more widely, white, able-bodied, educated heteronormative men are the locus of power. Characters in art (as in life) will talk about, and be concerned with, the actions of those who hold power – either over them or over others they care about. In societies where all spheres of power – business, finance, university research, the media, politics, law – are dominated by such men, as is the case in the UK and indeed much of Europe and the United States, attention will be disproportionately orientated towards the white male gender. This is not always because they are necessarily deemed more worthy of representation: it is also because in occupying certain social positions in a hierarchical society, they hold power over others' destinies.

That centralized male figure is, moreover, historically universalized: in Western literature, philosophy and anywhere – including children's literature – that a description of a human might be found. Therefore, he plays the unspoken norm against which all difference is implicitly produced – and the more ways in which a person's identity does not conform to that historically produced locus of power, the more likely their perspective is to be marginalized. Such identities include but are not limited to gender, including transgender and non-binary, race, class, sexuality, disability, neurodivergence, class, financial wealth/income, age and educational opportunity. Thus replacing, say, a white male protagonist with a Black female one in any given story structure cannot by itself reverse the underlying inequity in power relations. Nor does the fact of being female and/or any other marginalized identity, necessarily indicate antagonism to the dominant dramaturgical forms that privilege this form of power. There is currently a plethora of extremely successful, sharp-witted white female playwrights writing for London's major stages, who deploy with great dexterity the power dynamics expressed in what I've described as dramaturgies of winning and losing: a 'capitalist' framework for understanding character, agency and meaning.

To unpick how such dramaturgies can tend towards an impoverished representation of those who do not conform to social presumptions about what power looks like, I want to return to Noël Coward's riff on 'thin' – to look at 'thin' characters. If a play is 'thin' because its attention structure is at least as interested in its relation with the audience as in the rendering of an internally coherent 'world of the play', then a character might be deemed 'thin' when that character lacks depth or plausibility, existing primarily to enrich the portrait of another character. The American playwright Arthur Miller's plays express a deep lack of interest in, or sense of value of, female subjectivity, including (or even especially) in works in which women are central characters, such as in *The Crucible* (1953). This often goes unnoticed, given the precision of the dramaturgical structuring of attention towards male tragedy in family groupings. The character of Linda, wife of the protagonist in Arthur Miller's *Death of a Salesman* (1949), watches on helplessly as in scene after scene her menfolk play out an apparently inexorable tragedy of mismatched expectations. In Belgian director Luk Perceval's 2008 Berlin Schaubühne production, Linda was played with catatonic intensity by actor Carola Regnier. Barely moving, pushing to an extreme the lack of characterization, the production made her lack of agency unmissable – and showed it as an active force in a tragedy that as a result became hers, as well as the protagonist's. The lack of (female) agency was articulated by the production dramaturgy with the effect of intensifying the (male) tragedy – but also moving beyond the play's dramaturgy, by conveying the tragic subjectivity of the female character.

A variety of artistic strategies can be deployed to address or undermine or re-deploy the presumed values of the power relations expressed in any given play. That Miller's play was enriched in production by a critical relation to the weakness of its characterization of women is not to dismiss plays that are more interested in male characters. Rather it is to observe that the knock-on effect of the prevalence of productions of such plays, for a female actor, can be a lifetime of largely playing thinly drawn roles designed to illuminate the subjectivity of others – and that this is intersectional and therefore yet more extreme for female actors of, for example, global majority heritage. Such lack of complexity in female roles reduces the opportunity for actors tasked with playing those roles to develop their craft. Yet at the same time, one of the reasons, indeed, that thinness of representation is so often masked in production is not only that the play's dramaturgical focus is elsewhere, but also, ironically, because actors do extraordinary work in taking thin dramatic materials and creating from them complex, present representations in performance (labour that is intensified when other aspects of the actor's identity are also marginalized or unacknowledged by the work). This labour fleshes out the 'thinness', making roles written primarily as a foil to another character feel like dynamic figures in their own right.

This situation has not gone entirely unacknowledged in the professional theatre. One tactic has been to advocate for marginalized identities and create specific pathways towards greater representation in the workforce, on the assumption that parity in who is creating the work will lead to parity of representation. This is important, as who is in the room making the work is crucial – particularly for marginalized groups who are rarely represented within the stories that reach Western stages. The dramaturgical lens suggests, however, that this is only the start of a restructuring of power relations. With regard to the classical canon, for example, opening major roles to actors who do not match the supposed gender or racial identity of the character can seem like a panacea to the lack of depth and complexity of roles that are not coded white and male. However, if a production or process does not fundamentally interrogate the power relations within the work (or how that relates to contemporary societal power relations), what is asked of the actor – often unintentionally and certainly unspoken – is that they distort or discount the lived experience they might otherwise bring to the role and effectively play that role as though they were the white male it was written for.

Dramaturgies of imagining otherwise

But what might dramaturgies look like that do justice to temporalities and histories that do not either replicate or simply repudiate, as Caryl Churchill put it, 'the "maleness" of the traditional structure of plays, with conflict building in a certain way to a climax?' (quoted in Elaine Aston, *Caryl*

Churchill, 1997, p. 18). Whether this drive to achievement/ resolution in the arc of a play is seen as phallocentric, or indicative of the free-market economy's emphasis on winning and losing as structural values (or both, in combination), it only permits certain kinds of representation – forms of representation in which agency is taken for granted. For those in society whose agency is curtailed by racism, classism, sexism or ableism, in what forms can their/our experience be represented, without placing them/us as 'losers' in a relentless system?

Perhaps the most famous dramaturgical structure designed to create a recognition of historic systemic forces at work in the present, in ways that embed individuals in history and reveal that individual agency is part of a capitalist mythology, is in Churchill's *Top Girls* (1982). In the first act, famous women from different historical periods gather to celebrate Marlene's birthday – herself a cut-and-thrust businesswoman in Thatcher's newly neoliberal Britain. One sign of the act's dramaturgical force in situating all the female characters in the subsequent family drama as constituents of, and subject to, historical forces is that the specificity of Marlene's situation also marks her clearly as a character of her time, a very specific moment in the 1980s. This was a moment when individualism converged with careerism, and the autonomy sought by women for their bodies, relationships, working lives and creativity became conflated with a career-or-nothing culture, which radically emptied spheres of work traditionally gendered female of any vestige of perceived value or visibility.

The subject of debbie tucker green's *ear for eye* (2018) is the structural violence of racism, expressed through the dramaturgy, as well as in the content of its three very differently composed acts. The play uses historical document to dissect the active violence that constricts the lives of Black people living in cultures coded white as the norm. The first act, rather than telling a single story, refracts its point through multiple scenes of different scales and forms, each of which makes a searing statement about the violences that ensure that the status quo of white supremacy is upheld. Each of the vignette-scale scenes of the first act carries the weight of a short story in its spark of illumination, its light touch sharpening the pain of what is delineated, refusing the comfort arc of explanation and resolution. The twelve scenes are not arranged hierarchically to come to a climax of emotion but function accumulatively to suggest that the plethora of instances depicted is merely the tip of the iceberg. Any one of these moments could be the occasion for a whole play – but in focusing on multiple stories, the play forcibly expresses the criminal unexceptionality of the use and abuse of white power:

Scene Three.
UK.
Black British.

WOMAN   [. . .]
             When I was picked up and di'unt know
             why

and asked.
And asked.

When they told me I was
'bein aggressive'
when I weren't.

When they said I was shouting
when I was speaking
then changed it to I was
'acting aggressive'
when I weren't. I was just askin.
When they wouldn't answer me when I
asked them what 'acting aggressive' was.
When they changed it to,
I was
'talkin aggressive' which I weren't
when they joked, to themselves – not to me
– that we all sound aggressive to them
anyway. (p. 16)

The final act, in which a precisely lit triptych of pre-recorded films present Caucasian actors and non-actors, in different groupings, quoting the Jim Crow segregation laws in the United States, and the British slavery codes used in Jamaica, was seen by one theatre critic as detrimental to the force of the play, 'its deadening weight has the effect of lessening the dramatic vitality and momentum that the earlier parts have so brilliantly created' (Sarah Crompton,

'Review: ear for eye (Royal Court)', WhatsOnStage, 1 November 2018). However, through this dramaturgical refusal of, as Churchill puts it, 'building in a certain way to a climax' (Aston, *Caryl Churchill*, p. 18), the dramaturgy actively prevents completion or resolution – what the critic saw as flatness, in contrast to the 'lively' scenes before, is part of the play's political point. The codes of slavery and segregation are not simply a context from which to historicize the experience of the present; the values presented remain part of the unspoken fabric of contemporary Western culture.

Pattern and repetition allow themes to reverberate through the oeuvres of both tucker green and Churchill, deploying techniques that structure time and attention very differently from a narrative arc concerning the rise and fall of the hero. This is perhaps most searing in the mutating repetitions of a domestic scene in tucker green's *generations* (2005), with each new cycle lacking the next youngest character, as – beyond the scene and never mentioned by the characters – the AIDS crisis decimates South Africa. As an audience member, the belly punch of this dramaturgy, figured through the accumulated vanishing of the younger generation, remains one of my most intense theatrical experiences.

There are many kinds of dramaturgical strategies that do not seek to co-opt audiences' attention by inviting them to 'back' one character or another, get involved in second-guessing intention or encourage, as Brecht had it, 'eyes on the finish' (p. 65). Often such dramaturgies involve synecdoche (in which some part stands in for a whole), repetition, accumulation, substitution, parallels, hiatus – the silences, the pauses and the non-reciprocity of exchange between characters being louder at times than what is spoken. With many playwrights influenced by Churchill's use of punctuation to indicate ellipsis and overlapping speech, it has now become standard to use typography and grammar to enable texts to indicate expressive modes that intersect with, yet undermine, the supremacy of speech as a mode of communication. Many of these techniques are features of post-dramatic theatre, but rather than manifesting a reductive despair at the possibility of meaningful representation, the way that these techniques are used by Caryl Churchill and debbie tucker green (and playwrights in the United States such as Suzan-Lori Parks and Jackie Sibblies Drury or Elfriede Jelinek in Austria) makes a proposition not only for alternative dramaturgies but for alternative modes for understanding the world.

Theatre and climate crisis

Questions of representation – in relation to race, gender, sexuality, disability – have long been key to dramaturgical innovation in British theatre. But there is a new urgency to understanding the operations of dramaturgical form, for the global destruction of the environment has entered a critical phase, in which there is very little time left to alter the current direction of travel towards extinction. Much has been made of the difficulties of representation in relation to climate crisis, due to its extra-human dimension.

Indeed, the theatre and the dramaturgies that I've discussed concern themselves with human relations, to the exclusion of questions of the environment, except as backdrop, or at most, symbol (Una Chaudhuri, '"There Must Be a Lot of Fish in That Lake": Towards an Ecological Theater', 1994).

The question is often posed regarding what theatre, or dramaturgy, can 'do' in relation to the unfolding catastrophe of climate crisis. Plays of Churchill's, like *Love and Information* (2012) or *Escaped Alone* (2016), suggest that the classical male hero narrative is no longer fit for purpose in the information age – or in the face of environmental collapse. For decades, despite clear forecasts and elaborations of different potential scenarios in the public sphere, governments and other public authorities have themselves done next to nothing to alter a cultural and economic system that is plunging us into catastrophe. In fact, the rate of environmental destruction and the burning of fossil fuels have accelerated. Caught in a culture that encourages small-scale individual action over collective responsibility and systemic transformation, even advocates of political theatre feel somewhat helpless to know how to respond (I include myself in this). Too much, it seems, is asked of theatre in this context; expectations of inciting behaviour change at a personal level, of awareness-raising, make any given piece of performance feel inadequate to the gargantuan task of changing the social structure of a whole culture. In countless conversations and forums I've heard it argued that the issue is too complex, the landscape too vast, the timescale not that of two hours' traffic on a stage. Climate change is, supposedly, formally resistant to representation.

However, it is precisely on this front that novelist and essayist Amitav Ghosh refuses to let culture off the hook: 'The climate crisis is also a crisis of culture, and thus of the imagination' (*The Great Derangement*, 2017, p. 9). Ghosh's argument is that when it ignores climate crisis, culture participates in a kind of social silencing about what is facing the world:

> In a substantially altered world, when sea-level rise has swallowed the Sundarbans and made cities like Kolkata, New York, and Bangkok uninhabitable, when readers and museum-goers turn to the art and literature of our time, will they not look first, and most urgently, for traces and portents of the altered world of their inheritance? And when they fail to find them, what should they – what can they – do other than to conclude that ours was a time when most forms of art and literature were drawn into modes of concealment that prevented people from recognising the realities of their plight? (p. 11)

What Ghosh identifies as the cultural block that draws artists into these 'modes of concealment' is what brings us back to dramaturgy and specifically the way that traditional dramaturgies encode power relations in how they represent the person. What passes for realism in novels, according to

Ghosh, decisively characterizes humans as independent of, and in mastery over, nature. Yet what climate change means is increasing levels of deep unpredictability governing life, which Ghosh points out does not fit into the world of the realist novel, in the way that it knits together exterior events and the interior life of an individual central character. When used in novels (or indeed plays), climate disasters, beloved as they are of disaster movies, disrupt plausibility or seem overly evident as plot devices. The 'rationality' of classical dramaturgies implies a kind of incrementality, things changing in small steps that are clearly traceable to their causes and to who made it happen – not full-scale ruination utterly indifferent to immediate moral culpability.

A 3-degree centigrade rise in global temperature by the end of this century (the projected level of warming even if there is radical decarbonization in the 2020s) will bring with it increasingly widespread wars over basic resources of food and water, failing health systems and the mass migration necessary to avoid mass death. But if I look at it another way, from a less anthropocentric perspective, it could be said that climate change simply upends the dramaturgy of the human I've been describing, in flagrant disregard for its supposed dominance, with a storm-surge two fingers to the arrogance of the presumption that nature has been conquered.

So what rehearsals might we make for the future that aren't a smokescreen, that don't lie to us about who we might be? This is where performance dramaturgies might come in. In contrast with the 'rational economic actor' model of the human in growth-orientated global culture, who is 'self-interested, calculating, fixed in taste, and dominant over nature', alternative economist Kate Raworth suggests that people 'are social, interdependent, approximating, fluid in values, and dependent on the living world' (*Doughnut Economics*, 2018, p. 28). What does it look like to represent humans in this way? What dramaturgical forms enable us to understand ourselves as interconnected beyond the action represented in a theatre event? How might dramaturgy draw attention to otherwise unseen connections?

This notion of a relationally networked individual who is fundamentally collaborative means relinquishing certain ideas about our capacities for individualist action, about who we think we are and what it means to be a success. This relates not only to dramaturgical form and subject matter but also to how we go about the process of making theatre. The global coronavirus pandemic of 2020 threw the poverty of the old model of the individualist hero into sharp relief. At the start of the crisis, Spain's prime minister suggested that 'Being a hero is also about washing your hands, staying at home and protecting yourself in order to protect others' (Jon Henley and Sam Jones, 'Do Not Let His Fire Burn': WHO Warns Europe over Covid-19', *The Guardian*, 13 March 2020). This is the prosocial, networked person of Raworth's alternative economics. In the UK, healthcare workers expressed anguish at being called an 'angel' or a 'hero', rather than being provided with adequate protective equipment. The contrast between the high death rates in countries that relied more or less on 'survival of the fittest', compared with countries that sought to protect everyone, indicates that a dramaturgy of power that prioritized individualism over collective care fared worse.

Might this be a model for seeing a dramaturgy in the very structures of geopolitical responses to climate crisis? Are those of us living in industrial modernity going to continue to behave like the tragic heroes of classical dramaturgies, taking what's not ours to take (like Macbeth) or denying and delaying until it is too late (like Hamlet), clinging to cultural and economic individualism until we go down in flames, taking the planet with us? Or could we alter the dramaturgy? Could we see ourselves in another way, as part of an epic, unfinished story that none of us will ever see the whole of? Could we start to understand ourselves as co-dependent creatures with multiple pasts, and many potential futures that we can't predict but we can, collectively, work towards shaping?

This returns, in fact, to models of drama and dramaturgy long found in cultures across the world – and which were systematically outlawed as cultural practices by colonial settlers. Scholar and theatre maker Ngũgĩ wa Thiong'o offers a different story of drama, as arising from, and in symbiosis with, humans' ecological entanglements. Here dramaturgy still has humans and our representations at its heart, but includes the whole context of the life world we live within. It is worth quoting at length:

> Drama has origins in human struggles with nature and with others. In pre-colonial Kenya, the peasants in the various nationalities cleared

forests, planted crops, tended them to ripeness and harvest – out of the one seed buried in the ground came many seeds. Out of death life sprouted, and this through the mediation of the human hand and the tools it held. So there were rites to bless the magic power of tools. [. . .] Human life itself was a mystery: birth, growing up and death, but through many stages. So there were rituals and ceremonies to celebrate and mark [. . .] the different stages of growth and responsibility, marriages and the burial of the dead.

But see the cruelty of human beings. Enemies come to take away a community's wealth in goats and cattle. [. . .] There were also enemies within: evil doers, thieves, idlers: there were stories – often with a chorus – to point the fate of those threatening the communal good.

Some of the drama could take days, weeks, or months.

Decolonising the Mind: The Politics of Language in African Literature. London, 1986, pp. 36–7.

This pre-colonial form of drama is one that models interdependency rather than singularity and separation. It is one model among what must be a plethora of alternatives for forging dramaturgies appropriate to our times. As Aílton Krenak advocates in his published lectures, *Ideas to Postpone the End of the World* (2020), it is about embracing complexity and a fostering variety of stories – and dramaturgies. This is a part of what it takes to recognize ourselves – as citizens, as artists, as critics, as within and contributing to an ecosystem rather than seeking to impose a single model. Further, it is less about 'new' inventions and more about attending the wide variety of kinds of dramaturgy that already propose alternative ways of looking at the world.

I'd like to end with Amitav Ghosh's admonishment and call to arms in *The Great Derangement* (2017):

> When future generations look back on the Great Derangement they will certainly blame the leaders and the politicians of this time for their failure to address the climate crisis. But they may well hold artists and writers to be equally culpable – for the imagining of possibilities is not, after all, the job of politicians and bureaucrats. [. . .] What we need [. . .] is to find a way out of the individualising imaginary in which we are trapped. (p. 135)

Finding a way out of this 'individualizing imaginary' is what I believe the task of dramaturgy in the context of climate change is. It is something I've been working towards for the past few years, in a project of imagining life alternative economic conditions that has taken several different dramaturgical forms, including performance, theatre and installation. The project uses playful strategies to imagine what it would be like to live in a culture of ecological and social justice, a culture that took the climate crisis not as a problem to be 'solved' but as a fundamental demand to transform what we call 'high carbon culture'. 'High carbon culture' is the project's shorthand for the ecocidal entwinement of colonialism, capitalism and fossil fuel addiction that we, the makers, find ourselves bound up in. The project had its first public presentation as *WE KNOW NOT WHAT WE MAY BE* in September 2018, at the Barbican Centre, London, in a participatory performance installation that explored the potential for alternative futures structured through transformations in economics. The performance is described in detail in the final chapter of Lisa Woynarski's *Ecodramaturgies* (2020). Its latest incarnation was as a performance for *Re-EDOcate Me!* at the Floating University in Berlin (2022). This particular project places climate crisis centre stage, as the catalyst and condition of the work – but equally a performance might never mention climate breakdown, or address it as an 'issue', but be nevertheless responsive to the crisis: for we urgently need to rehearse models for how to work, live and survive *together*, in collaboration. As theatre makers, trained in the work of the imagination, it is up to each of us to invent our way out of the individualist trajectory of the tragic and instead to find a way to participate in transformation of our current challenges, on the scale of the epic. It comes back to the dramaturgical question: Will we in high carbon culture play the tragic hero and go down in flames, dragging everyone else and the planet with us, or can we change the dramaturgy? Writer Ursula Le Guin suggested something of what this might look and feel like in one of her last radio interviews:

> My guess is that the kind of thinking we are, at last, beginning to do about how to change the goals of human domination and unlimited growth to those of human adaptability and long-term survival, is a shift from yang to yin, and so involves acceptance of impermanence and imperfection, a patience with uncertainty and the makeshift, a friendship with water, darkness and the earth. (Radio interview, quoted by Zadie Smith, 'What Would We Be Like If Racism Never Existed?' *Vogue*, 4 June 2020)

Coda

Dramaturgy is the deliberate arranging of representational action in relation to time and space, which establishes a relationship with its audience. I have suggested that dramaturgy always has a politics, even if the theatre work being performed is not directly political: because dramaturgy delineates structures of power, in form and in its relation to the wider context of the audience. But might the theatre, in this deeply mediated age, have a political function just by existing? What does it mean to lay aside in the theatre for an hour or so the communication technologies that increasingly reduce the need for face-to-face relationships, in order to concentrate along with others on the same object, in the same place at the same time? Further, in an age of proliferating perceptual possibilities, what do the singular attention structures of theatre have to offer? Dramaturgy can help us to unpick the assumptions and affordances of making theatre in an increasingly complex and troubled ecology of life.

Last, but not least, is dramaturgy confined to the theatre? In what other arenas might a 'dramaturgy' be said to exist? It is my contention that 'dramaturgy' as a term is most useful when it isn't diluted. The presence or anticipation of an audience experiencing the work in the real time in which it is performed is what distinguishes dramaturgy from, say, the scenography of film. That the arrangement of the work is also intended to be representational also distinguishes dramaturgy from musical composition. However, political protest could be said on occasion to have a dramaturgy: recent performances of Extinction Rebellion participants, whose heavy make-up and vivid costuming, alongside a recognizable aesthetics of presentation in their slogans and imagery, seem to incorporate all the ingredients required for dramaturgy – being pre-planned and bounded in time and space by those specific actions – alongside being performed live for an audience (both present and through the wider media). Such performances of protest also have representational qualities – for example, the practice of organizing 'die-ins' at museums, shopping centres and outside financial services institutions, where large groups of people lie down on the ground for a set period of time, has become widespread as a way of representing contemporary violence – whether the violence of the climate crisis or the continued violence against Black people at the hands of police in the United States and the United Kingdom. Indeed, if relations of power can be made more legible by means of the dramaturgical lens, could the techniques of dramaturgy be usefully extended beyond the theatre: to enable a more nuanced understanding of the power relations in politics, economics and society – and, crucially, to devise the tools for creating alternative models for inhabiting the future?

further reading

Over the past twenty years, there has been a proliferation of engagements with dramaturgy in the anglophone sphere – in academia and in the professional theatre. The work of the Dramaturgs' Network (founded in 2001) has been key to developing the field. As a concept and practice that originated in continental Europe, the practice and theory of dramaturgy go back centuries – and many of the key thinkers on dramaturgy who have developed the field internationally, and in the UK, have European backgrounds. Importantly, they have also brought together a wide range of thought, collected in volumes such as Magda Romanska's *The Routledge Companion to Dramaturgy* (2014) and Katalin Trencsényi and Bernadette Cochrane's *New Dramaturgy: International Perspectives on Theory and Practice* (2014). If you read German, *Lektionen 1: Dramaturgie* (2009), a collection of essays relevant to dramaturgy gathered by German dramaturg Bernd Stegemann, is extremely comprehensive and a good place to start if you want to explore the histories and theories of European dramaturgy further. Sarah Grochala's *The Contemporary Political Play: Rethinking Dramaturgical Structures* (2017) is key for understanding how the form of a play is as political as its content. Cathy Turner and Synne K. Behrndt's *Dramaturgy and Performance* (2008) is excellent on both what dramaturgy *is* and what a dramaturg *does*. North American dramaturg Anne Cattaneo also examines the role of the dramaturg in *The Art of Dramaturgy* (2021). There are a wide range of books that aim to support playwrights dramaturgically – for example, David Edgar's *How Plays Work* (2009) and Steve Waters' *The Secret Life of Plays* (2010). Nicholas Ridout's *Stage Fright* (2006) and Dan Rebellato's *1956 and All That* (1999) are books I've returned to regularly for their dramaturgical thinking on the relationship between artwork and audiences.

A number of the books referenced here are from outside the sphere of theatre and performance studies – because understanding the structure of how audiences' attention is held in theatre is also a matter of understanding our social structures and expectations. Much of my understanding of European drama has drawn on Peter Szondi's *Theory of the Modern Drama* (1987) and Hans-Thies Lehmann's bible of dramaturgical features in *Postdramatic Theatre* (2006), which also has a lot that is useful to say about drama, as well as antagonisms to drama. Dramaturgy goes hand in hand with the spatial structures of performance and therefore also with architecture; Cathy Turner's *Dramaturgy and Architecture: Theatre, Utopia and the Built Environment* (2015) and David Wiles'

A Short History of Western Performance Space (2003) take a fruitful dramaturgical lens, such that their discussion of theatre spaces sheds light on dramaturgy, and vice versa. Last but not least, other editions in the *Theatre &* series go into much more detail regarding ideas and themes I've touched on here – in particular those on architecture, race, feminism, sexuality, entertainment, globalization, politics, feeling and ethics.

Bibliography

Aston, Elaine. *An Introduction to Feminism and Theatre*. London and New York: Routledge, 1995.

Aston, Elaine. *Caryl Churchill*. Liverpool: Liverpool University Press, 1997.

Auslander, Philip. *From Acting to Performance*. London and New York: Routledge, 1997.

Barish, Jonas A. *The Antitheatrical Prejudice*. Berkeley and Los Angeles: University of California Press, 1981.

Barthes, Roland. 'Diderot, Brecht, Einstein'. In *Image-Music-Text*, edited and translated by Stephen Heath, 69–78. London: Fontana Press, 1977.

Beckett, Samuel. 'Waiting for Godot' [1952]. In *The Complete Dramatic Works*, 7–88. London: Faber, 1990.

Bentley, Eric. *The Theory of the Modern Stage: An Introduction to Modern Theatre and Drama* [1968]. London: Penguin, 2008.

Bishop, Claire. 'Antagonism and Relational Aesthetics'. *October* 110 (Autumn), 2004: 51–79.

Bly, Mark. *New Dramaturgies: Strategies and Exercises for 21st-Century Playwriting*. London: Routledge, 2019.

Boenisch, Peter M. *Directing Scenes and Senses: The Thinking of Regie*. Manchester: Manchester University Press, 2015.

Bogart, Anne and Tina Landau. 'Preface'. In *Theatre & Feeling*, edited by Erin Hurley. London: Methuen Drama, 2010.

Bogart, Anne and Tina Landau. *The Viewpoints Book* [2005]. London: Nick Hern Books, 2014.

Bourdieu, Pierre. *The Field of Cultural Production: Essays on Art and Literature*, edited by Randal Johnson. Cambridge: Polity in Association with Basil Blackwell, 1993.

Bourriaud, Nicholas. *Relational Aesthetics* [1998]. Translated by Simon Pleasance and Fronza Woods. Dijon, France: Les Presses Du Réel, 2002.

Bratton, Jacky. 'What Is a Play? Drama and the Victorian Circus'. In *The Performing Century: Nineteenth-Century Theatre's History*, edited by Tracy C. Davis and Peter Holland, 250–63. Basingstoke: Palgrave Macmillan, 2007.

Brecht, Bertolt. *Brecht on Theatre* [1964]. Translated by John Willett. Revised ed. Tom Kuhn. London: Methuen, 2015.

Brecht, Bertolt. *Mother Courage and Her Children* [1939]. Translated by John Willett. London: Methuen, 1986.

Brook, Peter. *The Empty Space* [1968]. London: Penguin, 2008.

brown, adrienne maree. *Emergent Strategy: Shaping Change, Changing Worlds*. Chicago and Edinburgh: AK Press, 2017.

Campbell, Alyson and Stephen Farrier, eds. *Queer Dramaturgies: International Perspectives on Where Performance Leads Queer*. Basingstoke, Hampshire and New York: Palgrave Macmillan, 2016.

Cardullo, Bert and Robert Knoff, eds. *Theater of the Avant Garde, 1890–1950: A Critical Anthology*. London: Yale University Press, 2001.

Cattaneo, Anne. *The Art of Dramaturgy*. New Haven, CT and London: Yale University Press, 2021.

Chang, Ha-Joon. *23 Things They Don't Tell You About Capitalism*. Harmondsworth: Penguin, 2011.

Chaudhuri, Una. *Staging Place: The Geography of Modern Drama*. Ann Arbor, MI: University of Michigan Press, 1998.

Chaudhuri, Una. 'There Must Be a Lot of Fish in That Lake'. In *Toward an Ecological Theater*, 23–31. Durham, NC: Duke University Press, 1994.

Chekhov, Anton. *The Cherry Orchard* [1904]. Translated by Michael Frayn. London: Bloomsbury, 1995.

Churchill, Caryl. *Love and Information*. London: Nick Hern Books, 2012.

Churchill, Caryl. *Serious Money*. London: Methuen, 1987.

Cohn, Ruby. *From Desire to Godot: The Pocket Theatre of Post War Paris*. London: Calder, 1999.

Coward, Noël. *Design For Living* [1932]. In *Plays Three*, edited by Raymond Mander and Joe Mitchenson, 1–124. London: Methuen, 1979.

Coward, Noël. *Encore: The Sunday Times Book, Vol. 2*. London: Michael Joseph, 1962.

Coward, Noël. 'Introduction'. In *Plays Two*, edited by Raymond Mander and Joe Mitchenson, vii–xix. London: Methuen, 1979.

Crimp, Martin. *Attempts On Her Life*. London: Faber & Faber, 1997.

Crompton, Sarah. 'Review: Ear for Eye (Royal Court)'. *WhatsOnStage*. London, 1 November 2018. https://www.whatsonstage.com/london -theatre/reviews/ear-for-eye-royal-court-debbie-tucker-green_47932 .html.

De Angelis, April. *Interrogating a New Feminist Dramaturgy*. Ph.D., Royal Holloway, University of London, 2013.

Easterling, P. E. 'Form and Performance'. In *The Cambridge Companion to Greek Tragedy*, 151–77. Cambridge: Cambridge University Press, 1997.

Eckersall, Peter, Helena Grehan, and Edward Scheer. *New Media Dramaturgy: Performance, Media and New-Materialism*. London: Palgrave Macmillan, 2017.

Eddo-Lodge, Reni. *Why I'm No Longer Talking to White People About Race*. London: Bloomsbury, 2017.

Edgar, David. *How Plays Work*. London: Nick Hern Books, 2009.

Escolme, Bridget. *Talking to the Audience: Shakespeare, Performance, Self*. London and New York: Routledge, 1996.

Fisher, Mark. *Capitalist Realism: Is There No Alternative?* Winchester: O Books, 2009.

Fried, Michael. 'Art and Objecthood' [1967]. In *Art and Objecthood: Essays and Reviews*. Chicago and London: University of Chicago Press, 1998.

Ghosh, Amitav. *The Great Derangement: Climate Change and the Unthinkable*. Chicago: University of Chicago Press, 2016.

Graeber, David. *The Utopia of Rules: On Technology, Stupidity, and the Secret Joys of Bureaucracy*. New York and London: Melville House, 2015.

green, debbie tucker. *ear for eye*. Royal Court. London: Nick Hern Books, 2018.

Green, Jesse. 'The "Tina" Musical Is One Inch Deep, Mountain High'. *The New York Times*, 7 November 2019.

Grochala, Sarah. *The Contemporary Political Play: Rethinking Dramaturgical Structure*. London: Bloomsbury, 2017.

Halberstam, Jack. *Wild Things: The Disorder of Desire*. Durham, NC: Duke University Press, 2020.

Haraway, Donna J. *Staying with the Trouble: Making Kin in the Chthulucene*. Durham, NC: Duke University Press, 2016.

Harvie, Jen and Andy Lavender, eds. *Fair Play: Art Performance and Neoliberalism*. London: Palgrave Macmillan, 2013.

Harvie, Jen and Andy Lavender, eds. *Making Contemporary Theatre: International Rehearsal Processes*. Manchester: Manchester University Press, 2010.

Hegel, Friedrich. 'Tragedy as a Dramatic Art'. In *Hegel on Tragedy*, edited by Anne Paolucci and Henry Paolucci, 1–96. New York: Harper Torchbook, 1975, *c.* 1962.

Hill, Leslie and Helen Paris. *Performing Proximity: Curious Intimacies*. Basingstoke: Palgrave Macmillan, 2014.

hooks, bell. *All About Love: New Visions*. New York: HarperCollins, 2001.

Ibsen, Henrik. 'A Doll's House' [1879]. In *Four Major Plays*. Translated by James McFarlane and Jens Arup. Oxford: Oxford University Press, 1981.

Karoula, Rania. *The Federal Theatre Project, 1935–1939: Engagement and Experimentation*. Edinburgh: Edinburgh University Press, 2020.

Kane, Sarah. 'Phaedra's Love'. In *Complete Plays*, 63–104. London: Methuen Drama, 2001.

Karim-Cooper, Farah. *The Great White Bard: Shakespeare, Race and the Future of his Legacy*. London: Viking, 2023.

Kelleher, Joe. *The Illuminated Theatre: Studies on the Suffering of Images*. London and New York: Routledge, 2015.

Kershaw, Baz. *Theatre Ecology: Environments and Performance Events*. Cambridge: Cambridge University Press, 2009.

Kershaw, Baz. *The Cambridge History of British Theatre: Volume 3 Since 1895*, Cambridge: Cambridge University Press, 2004.

Kershaw, Baz. *The Politics of Performance*. London: Routledge, 1992.

Kershaw, Baz. *The Radical in Performance: Between Brecht and Baudrillard*. London: Routledge, 1999.

Laera, Margherita, ed. *Theatre and Adaptation: Return, Rewrite, Repeat.* London: Bloomsbury, 2014.

Lang, Theresa. *Essential Dramaturgy: The Mindset and Skillset.* New York: Routledge, 2017.

Lech, Kasia. *Dramaturgy of Form: Performing Verse in Contemporary Theatre.* London: Routledge, 2021.

Lehmann, Hans-Thies. *Postdramatic Theatre* [1999]. Translated by Karen Jürs-Munby. London: Routledge, 2006.

Lorde, Audre. *Your Silence Will Not Protect You.* Madrid: Silver Press, 2017.

Luckett, Sharrell D. and Tia M. Shaffer. *Black Acting Methods: Critical Approaches.* London and New York: Routledge, 2017.

Luckhurst, Mary. *Dramaturgy: A Revolution in Theatre.* Cambridge: Cambridge University Press, 2006.

Machon, Josephine. *Immersive Theatres: Intimacy and Immediacy in Contemporary Performance.* London: Palgrave Macmillan, 2013.

Martin, Carol. *Theatre of the Real.* London: Palgrave Macmillan, 2013.

McGrath, John. *A Good Night Out: Popular Theatre: Audience, Class and Form* [1981]. London: Nick Hern Books, 1996.

Miller, Arthur. *Plays: One.* London: Methuen, 1988.

Mitchell, Katie. *The Director's Craft: A Handbook for the Theatre.* London: Routledge, 2008.

Ngũgĩ wa Thiong'o. *Decolonising the Mind: The Politics of Language in African Literature.* London and Nairobi: James Currey/Heinemann Kenya, 1986.

Parker-Starbuck, Jennifer. *Cyborg Theatre: Corporeal/Technological Intersections in Multimedia Performance.* London: Palgrave Macmillan, 2011.

Perloff, Marjorie. 'Modernist Studies'. In *Redrawing the Boundaries*, edited by Stephen Greenblatt and Giles Gunn, 154–78. New York: MLA, 1992.

Phelan, Peggy. *Unmarked: The Politics of Performance.* London: Routledge, 1993.

Price, Jason. *Modern Popular Theatre.* London: Palgrave Macmillan, 2016.

Puchner, Martin. *Stage Fright: Modernism, Anti-Theatricality, and Drama.* Baltimore: Johns Hopkins University Press, 2002.

Radosavljević, Duška. *Theatre-Making: Interplay between Text and Performance in the 21st Century.* Basingstoke and New York: Palgrave Macmillan, 2013.

Radosavljević, Duška, ed. *Theatre Criticism: Changing Landscapes.* London: Methuen Drama, 2020.

Rancière, Jacques. *The Emancipated Spectator*. Translated by Gregory Elliott. London: Verso, 2008.

Raworth, Kate. *Doughnut Economics: Seven Ways to Think like a 21st-Century Economist*. London: Random House, 2017.

Rebellato, Dan. *1956 and All That: The Making of Modern British Drama*. London: Routledge, 1999.

Ridout, Nicholas. *Stage Fright, Animals and Other Theatrical Problems*. Cambridge: Cambridge University Press, 2006.

Romanska, Magda, ed. *The Routledge Companion to Dramaturgy*. London: Routledge, 2014.

Schechner, Richard. *Environmental Theater*. New York: Applause Books, 1994.

Shaw, George Bernard. *The Quintessence of Ibsenism*. New York: Brentano, 1928.

Shepherd, Simon and Peter Womack. *English Drama: A Cultural History*. Oxford: Blackwell Publishers, 1996.

Shevtsova, Maria and Christopher Innes. *Directors/Directing: Conversations on Theatre*. Cambridge: Cambridge University Press, 2009.

Sierz, Aleks. *In-Yer-Face Theatre: British Drama Today*. London: Faber & Faber, 2001.

Silberman, Marc, Steve Giles, and Tom Kuhn, eds. *Brecht on Theatre*. London and New York: Bloomsbury Methuen Drama, 2015.

States, Bert O. *Great Reckonings in Little Rooms: On the Phenomenology of Theater*. Berkeley, CA: University of California Press, 1987.

Stegemann, Bernd. 'On German Dramaturgy', translated by Johannes Stier. In *The Routledge Companion to Dramaturgy*, edited by Magda Romanska, 45–9. London: Routledge, 2014.

Stegemann, Bernd, ed. *Lektionen 1: Dramaturgie*. Berlin: Theater der Zeit, 2009.

Stein, Gertrude. 'Plays' [1935]. In *Writings and Lectures 1911–1945*, edited by Patricia Meyerowitz. Intro. Elizabeth Sprigge, 58–81. London: Peter Owen Ltd, 1967.

Stein, Gertrude. *Geography and Plays*. Madison, WI: University of Wisconsin, 1992.

Strindberg, August. 'Preface' to Miss Julie [1888]. In *Miss Julie and Other Plays*, translated by Michael Robinson, 56–68. Oxford: Oxford University Press, 1998.

Strindberg, August. *Letters to the Intimate Theatre*. Translated by Walter Johnson. London: Peter Owen, 1967.

Svendsen, Zoë and Simon Daw. *World Factory: The Game*. London: Nick Hern Books, 2017.

Svich, Caridad. *Toward a Future Theatre: Conversations during a Pandemic*. London: Bloomsbury, 2022.

Szondi, Peter. *Theory of the Modern Drama* [1965]. Cambridge: Polity Press, 1987.

Taylor, John Russell. *The Rise and Fall of The Well-Made Play*. London: Methuen, 1967.

Trencsényi, Katalin and Bernadette Cochrane, eds. *New Dramaturgy*. London: Bloomsbury Methuen Drama, 2020.

Trencsényi, Katalin and Bernadette Cochrane, eds. *New Dramaturgy: International Perspectives on Theory and Practice*. London and New York: Bloomsbury, 2014.

Turner, Cathy. *Dramaturgy and Architecture: Theatre, Utopia and the Built Environment*. Basingstoke: Palgrave Macmillan, 2015.

Turner, Cathy and Synne K. Behrndt. *Dramaturgy and Performance*. Basingstoke: Palgrave Macmillan, 2008.

Tyszczuk, Renata, Joe Smith, and Robert Butler, eds. *Culture and Climate Change: Scenarios*. Cambridge: Shed, 2019.

Waters, Steve. *The Secret Life of Plays*. London: Nick Hern Books, 2010.

Wilde, Oscar. *Plays*. Harmondsworth: Penguin, 1978.

Wiles, David. *A Short History of Western Performance Space*. Cambridge: Cambridge University Press, 2003.

Woynarski, Lisa. *Ecodramaturgies: Theatre, Performance and Climate Change*. Cham: Palgrave Macmillan, 2020.

Zola, Emile. 'Naturalism in the Theatre' [1881]. In *Theory of the Modern Stage*, edited by Eric Bentley, 351–72. London: Penguin, 1992.

index

4:48 Psychosis (Kane) 14
1956 and All That (Rebellato) 90

Abramovic, Marina 47
absorption/absorbed 26–30, 40,
    41, 44, 45, 53
absurdism 32
acting 15, 18–20, 23, 25
action 2–7, 42
'active' spectatorship 7, 49
actor 19–20, 22, 23, 25, 27,
    30, 35
Aeschylus 5
aesthetics 10, 28, 32, 43
'agitprop' theatre 45
alienation effect. *See* distanciation
All My Sons (Miller) 59
American Dream 58
Angelis, April de 46
anti-capitalist theories 39
anti-theatrical discourse 20
applause 26

Arden, John 42
Aristotle 4, 5
art 15, 23, 24, 30
    British 43
    contemporary 49
artistic practice 23
artistic strategies 71
Art of Dramaturgy, The
    (Cattaneo) 90
Arts Council 43
Arts Theatre 32
artwork 24–8, 32, 33, 35, 48, 49
Attempts on Her Life (Crimp) 14
attention, structure of 2, 26, 35
audience(s) 3, 8, 22, 33
    actor and 19–20, 25, 27, 35
    artwork and 48, 90
    attention 2, 6, 7, 9, 17, 21,
        27, 35, 41, 66, 90
    decision-making 52, 53
    dramaturgical relation
        with 15, 16, 86

emotion of   28
forms of theatre and   47–8
ignoring   25–6
relationship to
    representation   52
response   30
role in theatrical
    reception   31–2
auditorium   29–31
avant-garde   7, 8
Ayckbourn, Alan   18

Barbican Centre   85
Barish, Jonas   33
Barthes, Roland   25, 26
Beckett, Samuel   29, 32
Behrndt, Synne K.   90
Black Mime   44
Black Theatre Co-operative
    (nitroBEAT)   44
Black Theatre Forum   44–5
Bogart, Anne   1
Bond, Edward   42
Bourriaud, Nicolas   48, 49, 53
Brecht, Bertolt   39, 76
    legacy   41–2
Britain   42, 43, 73. *See also*
    United Kingdom (UK)
British Drama League   31
Broadway   61, 62
Brook, Peter   2

capitalism   55–8, 60, 65, 85
    bourgeois   59
    consumer   51, 52
    industrial   24
modern   60
neoliberal   42
racial   61–2
capitalist society   56, 60
capitalist system   45
Cattaneo, Anne   90
characters   5, 6, 10, 13, 19, 29,
    42, 53, 62, 67, 68, 70
Chekhov, Anton   30, 36, 58
Cherry Orchard, The (Chekhov)   30,
    58
Childress, Alice   61, 62, 64, 66
China   51, 52
chorus   5, 7
Churchill, Caryl   13, 42, 72, 73,
    76–8
City of London   50
Cixous, Hélène   46
class   44
    inequality   39
    oppression   37, 39
    struggle   45
climate change   10, 78–80, 84
climate crisis   77–86, 85, 87
Cochrane, Bernadette   8, 50,
    89
coda   86–8
collectivity   47
colonialism   56, 85
communism   45
Coney   50
*Contemporary Political Play: Rethinking
    Dramaturgical Structures, The*
    (Grochala)   90
control   44, 47, 57
coronavirus pandemic   81

Coward, Noël   18, 20–2, 30, 70
Crave (Kane)   14
Crimp, Martin   13–14
Crucible, The (Miller)   70
culture
    capitalist   59
    European   7
    financial   42
    high carbon   85
    relations   56
    renaissance   57
    specificity   7
    Western   55, 76

Daw, Simon   51
Death of a Salesman (Miller)   59, 70
Design for Living (Coward)   20
Devine, George   30
dialogue   5, 6, 11
die-ins   87
digital technologies   48
direct speech   29
disappearance   47
distanciation   41, 49, 53
Doll's House, A (Ibsen)   37–8
drama   3–8
    modern   15
    pre-colonial form of   82–3
    Romantic   17
    'slice-of-life'   36
dramatic structure   40
dramatic theatre   40
'dramatist-hypnotist'   48
dramaturg   9
dramaturgical structures   28, 49,
    56, 63, 73

dramaturgies of
    autonomy   15, 16,
        23–35
dramaturgies of
    entertainment   15–23
political dramaturgies   15,
    16, 35–48
dramaturgies of autonomy   15,
    16, 23–35, 43, 51
    absorption   26–9
    comforting convention   32–5
    ignoring audience   25–6
    legacies of Modernism   29–32
    Modernism   23–5, 27
dramaturgies of
    entertainment   15–23,
        35, 50
    acting for audience   18–20
    theatricality   20–3
Dramaturgs' Network   89
dramaturgy
    approaches   8–10
    architectural   43
    definition   1–3, 17
    of 'discussion'   37
    and drama   3–8
    European   90
    experimental   45
    interactive   50
    open/play   16
    and plays   10–12
    and production   12–14
    strategies   28, 76
    theatrical   61
    traditional   50
    winners and losers   57–60

Dramaturgy and Architecture: Theatre, Utopia and the Built Environment (Turner) 91
Dramaturgy and Performance (Turner and Behrndt) 90
Drury, Jackie Sibblies 63, 77
dystopian 52

ear for eye (green) 74
Ecodramaturgies (Woynarski) 85
economics
    contemporary 55, 56
    and dramaturgy 54–7
Eddo-Lodge, Reni 65
Edgar, David 42, 90
egalitarianism 47
embarrassment (embarrassingly lays bare) 24
empathy 59
Empty Space, The (Brook) 2
epic theatre 39–41
episodic form 41
Escaped Alone (Churchill) 78
ethnicity 44
Europe 4, 6, 9, 40, 45, 57, 58, 69
European Enlightenment 5
expert technique 22
exploitation 57, 59
Extinction Rebellion 87

Fairview (Drury) 63, 64
Federal Theatre Project 46
female
    artists 47, 71
    characters 68, 71, 73
    subjectivity 70

feminism/feminist 46, 47, 65, 67, 91
feudal system 56, 57
Floating University 85
fossil fuels 78, 85
'fourth wall' 25
France 5
Frayn, Michael 18
Freestone, Elizabeth 68
Fried, Michael 24

Gate Theatre 33
Gay Sweatshop 45
gender 44, 62, 72, 77
    categories 20
    identities 68
    white male 69
generations (green) 76
genre 12
geometric frame 26
German tradition 4
Ghosh, Amitav 78, 79, 84
Glass Menagerie, The (Williams) 6
global dominance 58
global temperature 80
Globe, the 10, 67
Good Night Out, A (McGrath) 38
Graeber, David 65
grand narrative 13
Great Derangement, The (Ghosh) 84
green, debbie tucker 74, 76, 77
Grochala, Sarah 90
Guardian, The 68

Hamburg National Theatre 4
Hamlet (Shakespeare) 67

Haraway, Donna J. 10
Hare, David 42
Hauptmann, Gerhard 36
Hegel, Friedrich 5
Henry V (Shakespeare) 57
heteronormative masculinity 59
Hill, Leslie 50
Holdbrook-Smith, Kobna 22
homophobia 18, 20
How Plays Work (Edgar) 90
human agency 17, 23

Ibsen, Henrik 36–8
Ideas to Postpone the End of the World (Krenak) 83
imagining otherwise dramaturgies 72–7
immersive experience 50
Immersive Theatres (Machon) 50
individualism 73, 81, 82
industrialization 58
industrial revolution 57
interactive and immersive theatre 16, 50
Italy 5

Jamaica 75
Jelinek, Elfriede 77
Jim Crow segregation laws 75, 76

Kane, Sarah 14, 33, 35
Kershaw, Baz 44
  theatre as disciplinary system 44
Krenak, Aílton 83
Kushner, Tony 42

Lady Windermere's Fan (Wilde) 19
landscape 28, 29
'la pièce bien faite' ('well-made play') 16–20, 37, 38
laughter 26, 35
Le Guin, Ursula 85–6
Lehmann, Hans-Thies 13, 90
Lektionen 1: Dramaturgie (Stegemann) 89
Lessing, Gottfried Abraham 3
Littlewood, Joan 42
live art 47
live performance 50, 87
Living Newspapers 46
Lloyd, Phyllida 22
Love and Information (Churchill) 13, 78

McGrath, John 38, 39
Machon, Josephine 50
marginalization 62–6
marginalized identities 71, 72
market economy 56
Marys Seacole (Drury) 64
middle class 37, 57
Miller, Arthur 58–60, 70, 71
Miss Julie (Strindberg) 26, 27, 58
Mitchell, Katie 30
Modernism 23–5, 27, 29–32, 48
Monstrous Regiment 45
montage 40, 45
Mother Courage (Brecht) 41
Mrs Warren's Profession (Shaw) 37

narrative 13, 29, 41
National Theatre 10
Naturalism 26–8, 36–9

New Dramaturgy: International Perspectives on Theory and Practice (Trencsényi and Cochrane) 8–9, 50, 89
New Wolsey Theatre 51, 68
New York Times, The 22
non-theatrical spaces 45

ontological queasiness 33
'other' 8

Paris, Helen 50
Parks, Suzan-Lori 77
participatory dramaturgies 48–53
   dramaturgical form 49–51
   politics 51–3
passive spectatorship 7, 49
people of colour 74
Perceval, Luk 70
performance installation 85
performances 2–4, 7, 8, 12, 15, 17, 18, 20, 22, 28, 30, 33, 45–7, 80
Performing Proximity (Hill and Paris) 50
Phaedra's Love (Kane) 33
Phelan, Peggy 47
plays 6, 7, 10–12, 15, 19–20, 28–9, 32, 33, 43, 56
'Plays' (Stein) 28
play-text 12
playwriting 29
plots 11, 18, 19, 29
political dramaturgies 15, 16, 35–48, 51–2
   Brecht's legacy 41–2

epic theatre 39–41
getting out theatre, performance and architecture of theatres 42–8
Naturalism 36–9
Politics of Performance, The (Kershaw) 44
Post-dramatic Theatre (Lehmann) 13, 90
power 54, 57, 60, 63, 66, 68, 70, 86–8
power relations 3, 10, 16, 65, 69, 71, 72, 79, 88
Private Lives (Coward) 21
productions 4, 9, 12–14, 22, 32, 34, 35, 43, 45, 46
protest 87
Punchdrunk 51

race 61, 77
racial identity 72
racial stereotyping 61, 62
racism/racist 61–3, 73
Rancière, Jacques 49
rational economic actor model 80
rational/rationality 55, 56, 80
Rattigan, Terence 18, 20, 30
Raworth, Kate 55, 80, 81
realism 36, 79
Rebellato, Dan 31, 90
Re-EDOcate Me! (2022) 85
Regnier, Carola 70
rehearsals 6, 7, 30, 61, 80
Relational Aesthetics (Bourriaud) 48

religious rituals   5
representation   2, 4–7, 13, 20,
        25, 26, 35, 36, 47, 53, 55,
        66–72
Resisters   46
Reza, Yasmina   18
Ridout, Nicholas   32, 33, 90
Romanska, Magda   9, 89
Roosevelt New Deal   46
Routledge Companion to Dramaturgy,
        The (Romanska)   9, 89
Royal Court   30, 32, 39
Royal Shakespeare Company   10

Sam Wanamaker Playhouse   10,
        67
scene   5, 6, 10, 11, 40, 41
Schaubühne   3, 70
Schneemann, Carolee   47
Scribe, Eugène   16
Second World War, the   43, 58
Secret Cinema   50
Secret Life of Plays, The (Waters)   90
self   35, 60, 65
Serious Money (Churchill)   42
sexuality   44, 77
Shakespeare   6, 22, 56–8, 67, 68
Shaw, George Bernard   17, 36, 37
Short History of Western Performance
        Space, A (Wiles)   91
slavery   75, 76
social inequality   45
socialism   40
social relations   25, 28, 48
solo feminist performance art   47
Sophocles   5

space   2, 4, 10, 11, 34, 86
spectacles   16, 25, 45
    participatory   51
spectators   2, 7, 20, 26, 33
Sphinx Theatre Company   45, 68
stage directions   11, 12, 29,
        30, 38
Stage Fright (Ridout)   90
Stanislavski, Konstantin   6
Stanislavskian rehearsal
        techniques   30
Stegemann, Bernd   3, 89
Stein, Gertrude   28, 29
Stevens, Tassos   50
Streetcar Named Desire, A
        (Williams)   59–60
Strindberg, August   26–8, 48, 58
surrealism   32
Szondi, Peter   90

Talawa   44
Taylor, John Russell   16
techno-capitalist system   53
technological modernity   23
Temba   44
text   4, 12
Thatcher, Margaret   42
Theatre & Feeling (Hurley)   1
theatre(s)   31
    buildings   43, 44, 46
    civic   4, 43
    and climate crisis   77–86
    companies   47
    contemporary   7, 23, 25
    culture   20
    etiquette   52, 63

European   16, 18
industry   4, 62
making   16, 81
participatory   50
political   15, 39, 42, 78
post-dramatic   13, 77
practice   23
site-responsive   50
site-specific   43, 50
street   45
theories of   40
types of   7
theatricality   15, 18, 20–4, 27
theatrical phenomenon   13
Theory of the Modern Drama
      (Szondi)   90
Thiong'o, Ngũgĩ wa   82
time   2, 4, 10, 86
time frames   11
Tina (2018)   22
Tonic Theatre   68
Top Girls (Churchill)   73
Trencsényi, Katalin   8, –9 50, 89
Trouble in Mind (Childress)   61–2,
      64, 66
Turner, Cathy   90, 91
Turner, Tina   22

UK Workers' Theatre
      Movement   45
United Kingdom (UK)   4, 9,
      53, 69, 81, 88, 89. *See also*
      Britain

United States   4, 6, 45, 46, 69,
      75, 87
urbanization   57, 58

virtuosity   15, 22

Waiting for Godot (Beckett)   29, 32
War of the Worlds, The (2022)   50
Warren, Adrienne   22
Waters, Steve   90
Weavers, The (Hauptmann)   36–7
Western industrial modernity   32
Western society   64, 65, 68
white gaze   64
white supremacy   62, 64, 74
*Why I'm No Longer Talking to White
      People about Race* (Eddo-
      Lodge)   65
Wilde, Oscar   18–19
Wiles, David   91
Williams, Tennessee   6, 59, 60
Winter's Tale, The (Shakespeare)   6
Women's Theatre Group   45
working-class   45
      life   39
      performance traditions   43
World Factory (Svendsen and
      Daw)   51–2
Woynarski, Lisa   85

Young Vic   10, 30, 51

Zola, Emile   36